HOW TO WRITE
A BLOCKBUSTER

HOW TO WRITE A BLOCKBUSTER

SARAH HARRISON

a&b

This edition first published in Great Britain in 1995 by
Allison & Busby
an imprint of Wilson & Day Ltd

Reprinted by Allison & Busby Ltd
114 New Cavendish Street
London W1M 7FD
in 1997

A catalogue record for this book is available from
the British Library.

ISBN 0 74900 197 6

Designed and typeset by N-J Design Associates
Romsey, Hampshire
Printed and bound in Great Britain by
WBC Book Manufacturers Ltd
Bridgend, Mid Glamorgan

CONTENTS

Tics.
Space for the imagination.
Breaking the veil.
'Murder your darlings'.

For the M.A.D. Writers

INTRODUCTION

Strange to relate, this is not the first or only book of its kind. Periodically some bright spark somewhere is persuaded to pop her head over the parapet and tell a waiting world how to write a bestseller. Will we never learn?

Apparently not. Among writers, the curious urge to pass on the lessons of experience is strong. And as for readers – well, hope, with ambition, springs eternal. As the latest in the line of public de-briefers, I'd like to clear one or two matters out of the way before I start.

For one thing, this is a book written from a writer's perspective. You could argue that there are an awful lot of others better equipped to talk about what makes a blockbuster – agents, publishers, critics, even booksellers. But on this occasion the task has fallen to me, and what I am qualified to talk about is the planning, researching, writing and promoting of a blockbuster novel from the author's point of view. I make no apologies for this, nor for the fact that I have not used interviews with any of the aforementioned experts in the course of this book. This omission is not through arrogance. I owe much of what I've achieved as a writer to the expertise of a terrific agent and a succession of first-class editors. I hope you'll grab with both hands any good professional advice which comes your way. But this particular batch is from Sarah Harrison, writer.

The very last thing I want to do is squash originality. But to produce this book I had to set certain boundaries, or we'd all have gone mad. Of *course* there are masses of 'wild card' novels which are also blockbusters – *Watership Down, Damage, Adrian Mole, The Hitch-Hiker's Guide to the Galaxy*. None of them conforms to any preconceived notion about bestsellers. And neither necessarily should you. This book is just a starting point. I hope it will provide you with a few ideas, some strategies, and at the very least the confidence to take the plunge.

In the interests of simplicity and consistency I shall be using the female pronoun throughout to mean both 'she' and 'he' when I refer to anyone who could be either. This is doing not what is politically correct, but what comes naturally.

Some of what's here you may have read before elsewhere. There's a certain amount of material which is common to almost every book, workshop, class, and lecture on creative writing. I've tried to be selective and use only what has a specific bearing on the blockbuster. If at any time I seem to be stating the obvious, skip it – all things are not obvious to all people.

In response to those who've asked me: 'Aren't you working yourself out of a job?', the answer is probably not, though it would be nice to think this book had been a help. Nor, as some have ventured to suggest, is this a deliberate exercise in misinformation. It doesn't need to be.

If writing a blockbuster were that easy, everyone would be at it.

1

YOU, ME AND IT

Welcome to the funny farm.

Yes, gentle reader, that does mean you. You may hitherto have regarded yourself as a serious person, but from the moment you bought this book (which if you're wise you have now put in a plain brown cover) you were sussed. You and I both know that you're a copy short of a boxed set – a megalomaniac in the grip of vaulting ambition and obsessive fantasy. Your friends may be too polite to say so, but they'll have noticed your glittering eye all right. Don't leave this lying around where any of them are likely to find it or your life won't be worth living.

If it's any comfort, you're not the only one. I must be mad too. As of now, we've entered into an unholy alliance designed to feed our shared delusions of grandeur. Let's make it our secret, shall we? And then when you've written your 1,000-page mega-seller you can pretend it just came to you, borne on a lightning bolt of inspiration, and pass me the used fivers in a carrier bag at a time and place convenient to us both.

'How to Write a Blockbuster'? I should ko-ko

Since I decline to spend the next 140-odd pages peppering my remarks with provisos, apologies and clauses intended to cover my back, let's get all that stuff out of the way before we go any further. This will serve the secondary purpose of testing your resolve – if you weaken you can flog this book to a susceptible friend without more ado.

1

So let's concede right away that:

● You can't write a blockbuster to order.
● Even if you do everything right there is no guarantee of success.
● A 'How To' book may put you in a creative straitjacket . . .
● . . . and it's naff.
● No single writer has all the answers.
● For every piece of advice given here there will be half a dozen opposite, contradictory and equally valid ones elsewhere.
● The whole enterprise is foolhardy in the extreme.

Let's dispose of these points one by one.

You can't write a blockbuster to order

Darn right, because a book can't properly be designated a blockbuster till after the event, i.e. till it's become a bestseller. On the other hand there's a lot you can do to reduce the risks and write a book that might, on a good day with a following wind, be a contender. Chapter Two is devoted to defining terms, so we won't get into that here. Suffice it to say that it's not my intention to give instructions – writing by numbers is the opposite of what we're after – but to put you in the right frame of mind, draw the parameters and provide an assortment of basic tools which you can either use or discard as you see fit.

Even if you do everything right, there's no guarantee of success

But then, is there ever? Look at it this way. If you *do* do everything right, your book may not be a blockbuster but it will almost certainly be a good read, assured of publication and a market, and with a respectable shelf life, none of which can be bad. If you aim high and fail, you're still likely to achieve far more than you ever thought possible.

A 'How To' book may put you in a creative straitjacket . . .

If you believe that, then your self-esteem is not sufficiently robust for you even to think of writing a blockbuster. What, you're just going to sit there and accept everything I say as though it were holy writ? Where's your spirit of adventure? One of the chief purposes of books like this is to give you something with which to disagree violently – a few hard, good-length shots off which to make punishing returns. There are times when you don't know what you think till you hear what you say. I'm finding that out as I write.

. . . and it's naff

That depends on how you make use of it. Let's reserve judgement till we've seen the results.

No single writer has all the answers

And I certainly don't claim to, as I hope I've made clear. My aim in writing this is to share my own experience and observations, and offer for your inspection such conclusions as I've been able to draw. I don't pretend to be anything but subjective.

For every piece of advice given here there will be half a dozen opposite, contradictory and equally valid ones elsewhere

Absolutely. There are as many views on writing as there are writers. Go thou forth and take account of them.

The whole enterprise is foolhardy in the extreme

Yup.

So that's that. And now, because there's no earthly reason why you should give any credence to what I say, it might help if I set out my stall.

Backing into the limelight

I always wanted to write (once I got over wanting to be Pat Smythe, from which you'll infer that I would not qualify for any list of 'young novelists'). The impression I get from talking to other authors is that this is untypical. Most writers, apparently, spend their time doing something else for the first couple of decades of their working lives, and then undergo some personal 'Road to Damascus' – redundancy? divorce? marriage? empty nest? – and come out of the closet.

Not me. My juvenile output was extensive. Not only was I prolific, I was the sunniest of optimists. And why not? A scribbling child enjoys one rare and priceless advantage – it's called Mum. This paragon reads everything you write with bright, adoring eyes and tells you it's wonderful. She means it. You believe her. Everyone's happy. In the normal course of events one would expect to lose for ever this invaluable captive audience – but at the age of nine I was sent to boarding school in Sussex and hit paydirt.

For here were 150 girls banged up in a top security establishment presided over by a *summa cum laude* graduate of the Mr Brocklehurst school of child psychology, with very little to read. Or anyway very little that they wanted to read. We were allowed to take back three books of our own each term and these were personally vetted by the aforementioned Head, who regarded anything remotely like a strong emotion or – Great Heavens! – a biological urge, as 'silliness'. She saw it as her sacred duty to confiscate at least two of these books, and you were left with the remaining one and the contents of the school library, which were relentlessly improving. As a result *Angélique* and her soul sister *Forever Amber* were our heroines. Beneath our blameless serge tunics, painting overalls and Viyella blouses were, metaphorically speaking, well-filled bodices, just waiting to be ripped . . .

It wasn't only the rumbustious social lives of these heroines we craved, it was their thrilling involvement in great events. Glittering courts, stinking underworlds, battles, schisms, mutinies and insurrections – you name it, our flame-haired gal was part of it, bosom heaving, green eyes flashing and libido in overdrive . . . In response, jaws tightened, eyes darkened, and manhoods quickened

4

orchidaceously at every turn . . . It was all so different, so *very* different from the home life of the average dorm prefect.

It's easy now to mock our breathless, girlish enthusiasm. But these were wonderful books by any standard, stories full of heroism and grandeur and grippingly well-told. This was long before the terms 'hot historical' and 'bodice ripper' became familiar to the reading public, but even today anyone who imagines that a fixed quota of explicit sex is a prerequisite of the blockbuster would be wrong. *Gone With the Wind* is one of the greatest ever popular novels because it combines stormy, larger-than-life relationships with an equally stormy period in American history. Powerful feelings are mirrored by powerful events and the characters' sense of their personal destiny runs in tandem with the destiny of a nation. Of strong passions and sexual attraction there's plenty, but of sex on the page, very little.

Signs and portents

Meanwhile, back at school, seeing that I had a large and eager potential readership, starved of entertainment and subject to social pin-down, I embarked on an amateur career which took me from the Lower Third to the Lower Fifth (a period of about five years) until the demands of 'O' Levels cut me off at the peak of my popularity. I filled dog-eared exercise books with the sort of stuff that I enjoyed reading: blockbusters. These were colourful stories about strong feelings, though where 'silliness' was concerned I had much recourse to that useful but now sadly unfashionable device, the row of asterisks.

I remember three stories in particular. One was set in Roman Britain. The garrison closely resembled nearby Roedean, where our first lacrosse team was trounced by their under-fifteens with deadly regularity. I eschewed sissy stuff like research, but being from an army family myself, I reckoned I did know how an army of occupation conducted itself, and what I didn't know I could readily imagine. The hero was a centurion, physically and emotionally scarred by years of campaigning in the service of some Caesar or other. He sought solace by indulging in that which my father had often inveighed against: 'fraternisation with women in garrison towns' (a multiple-asterisk activity). But when duty called, the centurion obeyed, with tragic results. It brings a lump to my throat just thinking about it.

The second story concerned a once-handsome young officer who returned blinded from some Far Eastern trouble spot in the 1950s to find his erstwhile sweetheart had taken up with his brother, an artistic type. He is comforted by another, stauncher female; his sight (and insight) are gradually restored and he falls madly in love with the jolly good sort who turns out to be twice as pretty as the first girl anyway.

The third story that sticks in my mind was based on an idea lifted wholesale from the cinema. The film in question was *The Singer Not the Song* starring the not-yet-ennobled Dirk Bogarde, mind-bogglingly tricked out as a cowboy. The distinguished actor appeared clad from head to toe in sprayed-on black leather, in which he resembled nothing so much as a shrink-wrapped Pontefract cake. He spent the whole film astride a white stallion for, I suspect, the excellent reason that any attempt to dismount would have involved an affront to public decency. I conceived a monster passion for Dirk in this sultry persona, and hastened back to school to make him the hero of my next opus. I have to say that my story was a great improvement on the film, being longer, juicier, and packed with incident.

You'll have realised that this was well before the days of feminist consciousness, political correctness, or any other inhibiting ideology. I mention this juvenile output only because of the huge pleasure I took in producing it and its astonishing success with the readers. Since I wrote the stories episodically (and usually illicitly) at the back of lessons, my audience was kept in suspense, looking forward keenly to the next instalment. And because I was cooped up with that audience for weeks at a time I had the sort of market feedback most sales directors would kill for. Looking back, that was a time when there was an unforced, felicitous fusion between what I wanted to write and what my readers wanted to read. Oh, happy days! I've always felt that fiction-writing is a branch of show-business or, to be more precise, of acting. That's partly to do with getting under the skin of the characters, but also with the fact that in my schooldays I had a visible, responsive, enthusiastic audience with whom I had a complete rapport. Now I'm a proper published author, it's what I miss most.

Introducing readers

At London University I produced only what was required to keep my fire-breathing tutor happy. But after university the writing bug returned and I spent several years on *Woman's Own* magazine. I began as a trainee, sifting through hundreds of readers' letters for the letters page. As the lowest form of editorial life I did not at the time realise that I was being vouchsafed a privileged glimpse into that secret and generally impenetrable place – the mind of the reader.

Readers are a strange species, their tastes unpredictable, their loyalties capricious, their very existence occasionally in doubt. But at *Woman's Own*, as I crouched Bob Cratchit-like over my desk in the main editorial office, surrounded by a log-jam of binbags stuffed to capacity with letters, I was in no doubt that this magazine *had* readers. Thousands of them – hundreds of thousands. And unappreciative though I was at the time, I was uniquely placed to get to know them. Behind the 'Was-my-face-red?' letters and the 'Things-they-say' letters and the'They're-almost-human' letters and the 'Believe-it-or-not' letters was an unseen host of individuals who together made up an amiable female giant – the *Woman's Own* Reader. She was a benign soul, aged somewhere between twenty-five and fifty, married with children, and while she might have a job (this was the mid-sixties), she was still home-centred. Flighty in my fun-fur, pvc boots and mini-skirt, and self-supporting in my Parliament Hill bedsit, I thought of the WOR as being different from me. But the merest scratch to my Biba make-up would have revealed the difference to be extremely superficial, as I was.

I began to feel a grudging affection towards the WOR and even gradually to identify with her. When the temporarily submerged desire to write fiction surfaced once more, to the detriment of my journalistic training, I found I quite naturally produced the kind

7

of stories, and the sort of storytelling voice, that was appropriate to the magazine. Small wonder, since I'd actually been paid to receive an extended seminar in addressing the market.

The breakthrough

The short stories in *Woman's Own* were to do with identification and empathy: the serials and serialisations were escapist. I drew no particular conclusions from this at the time, but looking back I can see that this fiction mix corresponds to that in the blockbuster novel: emotions that everyone can identify with, driving a story that is enthrallingly heightened.

After *Woman's Own* I spent a few years as a freelance, earning some money from writing magazine fiction and completing two novels which were very properly rejected by everyone in town. Then up rode the cavalry in the form of my inspirational agent, Carol Smith, who introduced me to editor Rosie de Courcy, who in turn pointed me in the direction of writing a historical novel – 'a First World War story with a women's angle' was the extent of the brief. What she had in mind was the sort of book I hadn't thought of writing since my schooldays – big, bold and expansive. Blockbusterish, in fact. I dithered, but with Carol's at times abrasive encouragement I submitted a synopsis, and a week later the novel was commissioned.

Frankly, my dear, I was scared silly. When I referred to my original synopsis my heart failed. What on earth had I let myself in for? Why the devil hadn't I opted for a slim volume of acerbic prose dealing with extra-marital shenanigans in NW3? Instead here I was, confronting this epic of 150,000 words (the publisher's suggested length), which had a cast of thousands, several foreign settings, a time span of twenty years, and involving enough historical research to ensure that I would be a stranger to daylight for many months to come. I could scarcely complain – it was all my idea.

On the other hand, nothing summons the literary muse more swiftly than a firm cash offer. Cautiously, trying not to look up at the mountain before me, I began.

In the event I wrote 260,000 words (useful, once read, as a doorstop or a weight for pressing tongue), they were delighted and it was all okay. Well, rather more than okay actually. Inclination, aptitude and opportunity had finally come together, and I'd written *The Flowers of the Field* – my first blockbuster.

One last thing while we're clearing the preliminaries out of the way. I have not written only blockbusters. Both *The Flowers of the Field* and its sequel *A Flower That's Free* qualify, but of the seven novels I've produced since, only *An Imperfect Lady* came close. It sold well, but did not quite make it, though interestingly it was the book I discussed most exhaustively beforehand with publishers (including those in New York). In retrospect I take this to be quite encouraging, since it all goes to show that there is something about the bestseller which defies analysis.

Make no mistake, every author wants every book she writes to be read by as many people as possible. No one sets out to write a book not caring whether it's widely read or not, and don't believe anyone who tells you different. But one may occasionally choose to write certain books which are directed at a more specific group of readers and which are unlikely by their very nature to be really huge, mass-market bestsellers – blockbusters.

I make no apologies for this. The fact that I've written blockbusters, non-blockbusters and one would-be-but-not-quite-blockbuster makes me well qualified to reflect on what it is that marks out the blockbuster proper.

And since I probably stand to learn more from writing this book than you do from reading it, I'm optimistic for the future.

2

BIG STUFF

So what busts the block?

We've established that the term 'blockbuster' can only truthfully be applied to a book after it's become a proven success. But we can pinpoint certain attributes which all blockbusters have in common. A good way to start is by reading a few. If that idea engenders even the faintest distaste, or carries with it the merest suggestion of 'slumming', forget it.

Most books on writing for publication stress the importance of market research, and I go along with that up to a point. The difference here is that the 'market' we're addressing is (we hope) the entire English-speaking world, and that's just for starters. So what we're looking for is something more radical, but also harder to categorise, than the criteria for, say, a magazine short story.

First of all, can you yourself recognise a blockbuster? Try. Go into a bookshop and look along the shelf. Have you heard of the author? Does the title of the book ring a bell? What does the book look and feel like? This may all sound superficial, but remember we're working backwards here, trying to establish retrospectively what has got this book where it is today.

I suggest that the first thing you'll notice is that it is BIG.

Big in size

As the term suggests, the blockbuster is a thumping great book. I'll even stick my neck out and say that it's going to be somewhere between 450 and 800 pages. There are plenty which are much longer – those in the James Clavell *oeuvre*, for example – but I don't want to intimidate you.

Okay, I hear you cry, but what about all the bestsellers which are nothing like that length? What about the novels of Sue Townsend, Joanna Trollope, Mary Wesley, Douglas Adams? There is, as Eric Morecambe used to say, no answer to that. All those books are brilliant, idiosyncratic works of fiction which found their moment and their audience. They're undoubtedly bestsellers and in some cases mould-breakers which created new genres. The term 'blockbuster' is not a genre but a classification. You can't legislate for lightning.

To return to size – I wish I had 10p for every person who comes up to me and says: 'When are you going to write another of your *big* books? I do love a nice, long book, something that lasts, something I can get my teeth into, something I don't get through too quickly . . . ' On and on they go, rhapsodising not about characterisation, plot or style, but the virtues of sheer, brute size. It happens too often to be ignored. If opening a book is like opening a door on to another, magical country, then the bigger that country is, the greater the magic. Only a snob would dismiss the visceral delight to be had from the mere handling of an opulently thick book, with its promise of many good things.

What the blockbuster must do is fulfil that promise.

Big in appeal

The blockbuster sells millions of copies, and in order to do so it must have appealed to millions of people.

But don't assume that this means going for some wishy-washy, lowest-common-denominator kind of approach. On the contrary, it's essential to have ideas above your station. Be grand, be daring, get thoroughly above yourself. It's the property of all novels to give personal thoughts, emotions and behaviour a universality, and this is specially true of the blockbuster. Your story must have real emotional experience writ large, so that the reader at once identifies with it but is lifted out of herself.

A blockbuster novel has glamour, in spades. That doesn't mean nubile lovelies in satin scanties, and saturnine studs lithe as panthers – though they can be there if required. No, I mean glamour in the sense of absolute, undeniable, gobsmacking allure. This is not a quiet little mouse of a book, full of good qualities but too shy to parade them. It's a bold, warmhearted, expansive book that bursts upon the consciousness and the imagination with all the maidenly restraint of Joan Collins on speed. An old-fashioned movie star of a novel, aware of its responsibility to please and confident of its ability to do so.

Look at *The Thorn Birds*. Here is Colleen McCullough's deeply personal memoir of her mother, and life on an Australian sheep station. Her memories of her family, and of the farm and the country where they lived, give the story a grainy authenticity. Against this the author sets the lifelong love affair between Meggie (only a child when the story opens) and the Roman Catholic priest Ralph de Bricassart. The author leaves us in no doubt that we are in the presence of doomed transcendent passion. And as anyone who's read the book knows, you'd have to be made of stone not to have your withers wrung by the lovers' predicament.

Tensions are set up early. Ralph may be sworn to celibacy, but he's drop-dead sexy, and unselfconsciously hoists his soutane to dance the Black Bottom at an outback knees-up. Later on, as a bishop, he even rattles up to visit Meggie driving a Dodge and wearing ragged shorts. His vocation may be priestly, but his nature is robustly masculine and physical.

As for Meggie, because she's only a child when she and Ralph first meet, there is a double prohibition on their powerful mutual attraction. And because their love is forbidden, with all the spiritual, emotional and physical anguish that entails, it remains long unfulfilled. There is scope for it to ring down the years, encompassing Meggie's marriage to another man, the birth of her two children and Ralph's elevation to cardinal.

This is one of the great fictional love affairs. And in the farm, Drogheda, Colleen McCullough creates one of those places like Manderley and Tara which live on in the mind – a place that is just as much a player in the story as any of the human characters.

The strength of *The Thorn Birds* is that while we may know nothing about the place, the period or the predicament it describes (this is the escapist element), we can all identify with the emotions which drive the action forward. There is an awesome inevitability in the unfolding drama, which does not detract from the narrative tension, but makes us turn the page with a thrilling sense of the characters' destiny at work.

The much-satirised, hackneyed line of screen lovers, 'This thing is bigger than both of us', could easily apply to the blockbuster. It must brook no argument, but sweep us off our feet.

It's big stuff.

Big in scope

In the previous section I mentioned that Colleen McCullough makes Ralph and Meggie's love a lifelong one. It's therefore likely that although the geographical roots of the story are in the Australian outback, these two characters, their ancestors and their descendants, will live in, and travel to, many other places. The author gives her story a broad canvas. Even if you don't choose to cover many years and many miles, your story must carry a sense of its own wider implications.

The trouble is that many of the adjectives associated with the blockbuster have become devalued by over-use in innumerable paperback blurbs. Epic, panoramic, breathtaking, sweeping, timeless . . . You could probably add several more. But the message is there. There has to be a sense of the great scheme of things unfolding before us.

A big step

The Flowers of the Field involved a huge change in my attitude towards my writing. At the time of starting I had never written anything over 100,000 words. The stipulated minimum length for this was 150,000 words (for the uninitiated that's about one and a half inches thick). The brief, remember, was for a First World War novel with a woman's angle. My editor wanted a big, sweeping canvas against which a compelling personal story would be played out.

Obviously the background would be a key ingredient in the book. But since the characters and their story were paramount, I had to find a way of using the background to maximum possible effect without overshadowing them.

What I did was to make the story of the Great War into the characters' story too. As I was a rank beginner in the writing of historical novels, this was a relatively straightforward and effective way of making sure I did justice to the period while retaining the characters' integrity. It involved the tying in of real and imagined events – a wild elopement just before the outbreak of war; a frantic search through the streets of Paris as war breaks out; the meeting, during the Christmas fraternisation of 1914, of two men who are unaware that they love the same woman.

Characters are fundamental to the appeal of any book – it's not overstating the case to say they *are* its appeal. The 'women's angle' was a given. I wanted a strong, sympathetic heroine (always tricky – more later), but it occurred to me that one or two supporting female players would provide different perspectives on this very turbulent time. A sister, perhaps? Or a friend? A sibling has built-in dramatic possibilities – family tensions and loyalties, and the ever-present shared past. But in many ways a friendship is a stronger influence than a blood relationship. A friend is chosen. The problem with both of these was that they would by definition come from the same social background as the heroine. At a time when the English class structure was at its most rigid (but about to be given a massive shake-up), it would be interesting to have a different social point of view. So to my two sisters I added a parlourmaid who worked in their household, and whose position *vis-à-vis* her employers would change radically as a result of the war.

I did keep the friend, but in a more peripheral role. Now I had three women poised to experience tumultuous change in very different ways.

My heroine, Thea, becomes involved in the Women's Suffrage movement and subsequently trains as an ambulance driver and goes to France in that capacity. Her younger sister, Dulcie, is a flighty piece who wants it all without working for it, and who exploits the situation according to her talents. Primmie the maid, hardworking and singleminded, becomes a nurse.

14

Since it was never likely that these women were going to live like nuns, it followed that there would be strong male characters, too. But the role of the men in *The Flowers of the Field* was not simply to provide romantic interest. A blockbuster set at the time of the Great War must not be afraid to show the war at first hand. My book needed a presence in the trenches on the Western Front. So my hero, Jack, is an army officer, only removed from the front line when he's shot down by a sniper's bullet at Ypres. The girls' brother, Aubrey, is also an officer, but is taken prisoner at Mons and spends the remainder of the war in a prisoner-of-war camp. Their shy, intellectual cousin becomes a conscientious objector. And there is a Beloved Enemy, Josef – an Austrian aristocrat with whom Thea falls hopelessly in love before the outbreak of war.

I deliberately began the book with Thea's birth so that the reader knows her from the start, and knows, too, that her life will be profoundly affected by what lies ahead.

If all this sounds cold-blooded or mechanistic, it wasn't. What I'm doing here is analysing in retrospect what I did then. At the time I simply knew what kind of book I wanted to write, and set about it with a burning desire to tell the story, and the conviction that I was embarking on something enormously exciting.

Pow! Big impact

Blockbusters pack a punch. 'Powerful' is another of those adjectives often used to describe them. But 'power' is a hard thing to define in a novel. It's a combination of strong, expressive writing and gripping subject matter – the kind of storytelling which grabs you by the throat on page one and keeps you riveted and involved to the last. The reader willingly submits to the power which the author has over her.

It's easy to say what is *not* powerful:

- Half-hearted descriptions, whether of people, places or events.
- Jokiness (*pace* Jilly Cooper, a special case).
- Evasiveness in carrying through plot-lines – short-changing the reader.

- Insufficient depth and texture in the characters or setting.
- Half-heartedness.
- Apparent lack of confidence.

I left the last two till the end because they're usually connected, and because they can be the hardest problems to overcome. Half-heartedness often results from lack of confidence – the 'nothing ventured, nothing lost' mentality that's death to blockbuster-writing, which requires you to think BIG and to ask not 'Why me?' but 'Why not?' I hate to stereotype, but adopting this attitude is akin to pulling teeth for the British. We have an innate sense of irony which prevents us from taking ourselves completely seriously. I like irony myself, both as a reader and as a writer. You'll see I black-listed 'jokiness' rather than irony or humour, because I think a story without these two makes for a lifeless, unaffecting read. But I think one has to be aware of the dangers. Irony *can* distance the writer from her subject-matter because it plays on the existence of a double agenda.

It's un-English to go for it, but do it anyway. Only your nearest and dearest have any preconceptions about you, and they'll get over it.

I was given a swift lesson in self-esteem by my first-ever American publisher, a cruiser-class Manhattan lady in a sable coat and diamonds as big as Bergdorf Goodman, who at our first meeting wrung my hand and pronounced sonorously: "Sarah, I adore this book! It has *tripartite sensibility*." Wow, it did? Could she mean me? I couldn't have liked it more, though I've never quite summoned the nerve to use the phrase since. She went on to describe my dialogue as "exemplifying the eloquent ellipses in British upper-middle-class social intercourse . . . " Gosh. A bit over the top, but jolly gratifying. Her remarks displayed a robust disregard for the division between the 'literary' and the 'popular', which frankly we could do with a bit more of this side of the pond.

And while we're talking of power, impact and thinking big, perhaps this would be as good a time as any to mention the title.

The big banner

I'm a great believer in the potency of titles. In fact they're so important to me that I like to have them in place first, preferably before I start on any detailed planning, and certainly before I begin writing the novel.

The cover and the title together make up the blockbuster's initial siren song to the customer (who at this stage *is* the customer – not yet committed to reading the book). In seconds, and in no more than a few words, it must convey the feel, the 'taste' of your book. A good title must set the reader's imagination on a particular tack, but also have 'spin' – offer other possibilities for the imagination to work on.

By and large a title of more than one word works better (though one immediately recalls *Dynasty, Lace, Riders, Rivals, Polo,* not to mention *Angélique . . .*). Some degree of familiarity is often helpful because it gives the imaginative process a kick-start. This is why so many titles are quotations. Some say the reason the Desert Island Discs castaways are given the Bible and Shakespeare is so that they can think up titles for novels. Both are a rich source of ringing phrases which combine the familiarity of race-memory with the mystery and music of great language.

As that New York editor might have said, multiple resonance is what we're after here. *The Flowers of the Field* was a title which sprang fully formed on to the page, in fact those were the first five words I wrote, at the top of the initial synopsis which Carol Smith sent to Futura Publications. And I still think it's a good title. It's worth analysing why.

For one thing, the image of flowers, along with 'the field' of battle, conveys the idea of women in time of war. And who doesn't at least half-remember that line: 'In Flanders fields the poppies blow . . . '? No other war has been so closely associated with one particular flower, and the humble blood-red poppy has become a potent symbol of sacrifice and remembrance. The title also carries a hint of the famous Highland pipe lament, *The Flowers of the Forest.* And then there is the echo of the funeral service in the Book of Common Prayer, with its idea of man as a flower which blooms, withers and is cut down . . . Tripartite sensibility? At least.

17

The Wind Cannot Read and *Gone With the Wind* use the idea of a powerful natural force sweeping all before it. Both suggest the wasteful and arbitrary carnage of war, and the transience of human concerns.

The Thorn Birds is striking and enigmatic. Thorns are painful and constraining: birds are wild and free. A tension is set up. On the flyleaf we are told that the thorn bird only sings when it is dying, like the swan, and that its death, impaled on a thorn, is self-inflicted. The whole tenor of the story is encapsulated in the title.

Bear in mind sayability. Your blockbuster will depend for a large part of its success on word of mouth. For this reason foreign words and phrases may not be a good idea. I wanted to call a novel *Fin de Siècle* but the title was scotched, quite rightly I now think, because many people might have been self-conscious about asking for it. On the other hand, *Sayonara, Taipan* and *Shogun* – all Japanese, interestingly – while we may not know what they mean, are easy to pronounce.

My second novel, sequel to *The Flowers of the Field*, is called *A Flower That's Free*. In several respects this is a good title: it contains an echo of the first; the word 'free' has spin; and it's a quote from 'London Pride' out of Noel Coward's patriotic show *Cavalcade*. Where it fell down was on sayability. It was a little too like the first, with its alliterative 'F'. And all those contiguous consonants are awkward.

So think hard about your title. It must catch the eye; it must inform, but only just enough; and it must engage the imagination – all in seconds.

Big in heart

Well, shucks, I don't want to make too much of this, but . . . you've got to *love* your putative blockbuster. Be *in* love with it, even. You cannot be cold-blooded about writing a blockbuster. The various acquired skills which make up the craft of writing are all useful tools – but writing is also an art, not to mention a passion. The tools are not the thing itself. The best writing has at its heart a spark of individual creativity, an X-factor which makes it unique and cannot, thank God, be taught. A gifted editor once told me that what she most looked for in a new writer was 'the glint of obsession'.

Never, *never* be condescending towards your audience. The blockbuster is aimed at the biggest and widest possible readership – the mass market. But that mass is made up of individuals like you, and me, and the girl on the check-out and the college lecturer. It is both a privilege and a responsibility to attempt to reach and engage such a diversity of readers. If you feel, even for a moment, that you are writing 'down', then stop. You've got it all wrong. You're demeaning yourself and insulting the very readers you hoped to seduce. What we want and expect when we buy a blockbuster novel is what the Americans call 'a class act', and you had better not disappoint.

This is not the time to be niggardly, mean-spirited or over-cautious. You have to go for broke. Time enough for a healthy scepticism when the publicity wave breaks over your head – but more of that anon.

Your book should have a big heart, and so should you. You're going to need a more-than-averagely generous spirit to rise above your inevitable detractors. If your blockbuster succeeds, both it and you will instantly be high profile, and high profiles attract criticism. Try to think positively. You've done your best, and now all publicity can only be good publicity. You may feel like having a damn good howl, but for heaven's sake do it in private. Nothing's worse than a successful and well-rewarded person whingeing on about the downside of fame and fortune, no matter how true it may be.

As well as criticism, there's jealousy. This is harder to cope with because there's no rational argument against it. You just have to be big enough not to let it faze you.

After all (you must be able to say), who got out there and did it? You, or them? Well then.

I hope that by this time you can feel your lungs expanding, your heart pounding, and your imagination firing on all cylinders. If so, terrific – hang on to that feeling. Writing a blockbuster is incredibly hard work, but if you can keep the excitement going it will make the bad times easier and the good times brilliant.

Shall we go through?

3

THE LIGHT BULB: IDEAS

You know the scenario. The penniless novice writer sits in her attic/cellar/Hebridean croft/leaky houseboat on the Great Ouse, hunched over her lined notepad, pencil stub clasped between fingers blue with cold, stomach rumbling with unassuaged hunger, mind as blank as the page before her. She has renounced all in the service of her art – family, friends, job, the everyday comforts of her life in the ordinary world. But a year has gone by and as yet she has written nothing of the least merit, value or interest. Actually, she has written nothing.

She is in despair.

Then all of a sudden, something happens! A shaft of light penetrates the murk of her uncleaned window and dispels the gloom within. It falls upon the bowed head of the writer and illuminates the empty page before her. Down this shaft of light with draperies a-flutter glides the Literary Muse, fairy godmother to our scribbling Cinderella. Brushing our heroine's brow lightly with her quill she ignites the flame of inspiration. The room, not to mention the writer, brightens visibly. The pencil begins to move across the page as though of its own volition, at first slowly but with ever-increasing speed and confidence . . . The work has begun.

Good, eh?

In your dreams

For a start, most writers find the world is too much with them. Far from being shut away in some secret and inviolable place of their own, they are usually contending with a full complement of external pressures, not to mention the myriad petitions of conscience (which always pertain to things other than the work in progress). With all this going on it's hard even to recognise a brilliant idea, let alone hang on to it.

20

In my experience ideas don't submit easily. The light bulb does not come on with sudden, steady brilliance. The effect is more like the stuttering flicker of an ancient striplight, grudging and tantalising, and also like the ancient striplight it may at last come on – or blow, and fuse the whole house.

Here's another metaphor. Ideas have to be stalked. They are fey, retiring creatures like unicorns, grazing deep in the undergrowth of the subconscious. Nor is it very likely that an idea, once laid hold of, will be complete. It's more likely to be a piece of the whole, whichever part of the unicorn we happen to have touched. You need to supply more, explore the idea, approach it from different angles, until eventually you form a complete picture of what it is you have in your grasp.

Where do ideas come from?

They're 'out there', you're aware of them but they elude you. The important thing is to note all sightings, and develop a sort of mental box-room or cupboard-under-the-stairs into which all snippets, traces, glimpses and merest whiffs can be stuffed till they're needed. You'll notice I said 'mental' because I personally have never in my life actually noted down a decent idea when it occurred to me. I don't present this as a virtue, just as a fact. I never have a piece of paper to hand when these notions present themselves, and I'm blowed if I'm going to cart a notebook everywhere (it makes other people nervous). As for bits of scrap paper out of one's handbag or pocket, no matter what gems may be jotted on them they tend to get returned whence they came and once more become bits of scrap paper to be chucked in the swing-bin during the next great handbag-and-pocket blitz . . . I have, however, cultivated the ability to stash away unconsidered trifles in the mental box-room. You can then go and have a good rummage around when circumstances dictate.

This jumble of the imagination can be culled from anywhere. A place, a person, a situation, a story in the newspaper or on television – but the best source as far as I'm concerned, and this goes for all novels, not just blockbusters, is conversation. This may be quite simply because *The Flowers of the Field* was the result of a conversation, and I nurse some subliminal, superstitious notion that this will be the route to further success. Or it may be that I'm a nosey so-and-so, always on the *qui vive.*

It's those chance remarks that are like snapshots, or a glimpse through half-closed curtains, which give you the sense of a whole contingent story not yet revealed. But here again we have to separate out the blockbuster as a thing apart.

For instance, I was recently in conversation with my niece, a young woman in her twenties who, with her partner, is about to acquire and run a pub. In the course of enthusing wildly about a line of business which I would pay a king's ransom to avoid, she mentioned quite casually that one of the chief reasons pubs came on to the market was the break-up of the marriage or relationship of the existing owners. In other words, the pub trade is like showbusiness – packed with temptation, unsocial hours, spurious glamour and gruelling hard work. It places enormous strains on the people concerned. As often as not, my niece told me, one half of the partnership cracks under the strain, or starts an affair with a customer and whoosh! – end of cosy idyll. Now I'm fairly certain that sometime, somewhere along the line, I shall make use of this. It might be the basis for a whole novel or just part of one. But a blockbuster it isn't.

Here's one that is, though. Expand that earlier idea. What if the place is not a pub (or only to begin with) but a hotel, then the smartest hotel in London, then a whole group of hotels in the great capitals of the world? What if the couple who split up run rival hotel chains? What if one of them falls on hard times and goes to work incognito for the other with a view, eventually, to usurping her? Get my drift?

Here's another. During the events marking the fiftieth anniversary of D-Day in 1994, several newspapers ran the story of a veteran who on returning to the area in northern France where he had landed fifty years before, went to honour fallen friends buried in the local cemetery. There he was shocked to discover his own grave.

Now that, for me, has everything – history, remembrance, romance, mystery, boundless opportunities for drama and intrigue and a rich choice of periods and places. *That*'s a blockbuster.

Time

It may be that you're itching to write about a particular period. Perhaps you're passionate about the English civil war, or the Crusades, or the sixties, and that passion may well be the fertile ground in which a blockbuster can grow. But remember – an exhaustive knowledge of the period is not enough to make a compelling novel (nor, incidentally, unless you are the greatest living expert, is it likely to produce a great new history). First and foremost you must have a wonderful, unstoppable story and powerful characters.

As a general guideline – though as with everything the publishing world remains to be pleasantly surprised – stories set in pre-history are a liability, for reasons of empathy. It's difficult for a reader to identify with a hero who communicates mainly through his club (I don't know though . . .) and has no language in the modern sense.

For the same reason, the blockbuster does not naturally flourish in the future, or entirely in the realms of fantasy. I realise I'm on shaky ground here, because where does that leave the novels of Douglas Adams? And Terry Pratchett? Not to mention Richard Adams? And Brian Aldiss? They are books in which the X-factor worked like strong drink on the book-buying public. But not all of us possess the X-factor to quite that happy extent. In this book we're trying to discount the effect of the X-factor as much as possible, so that if you find you have it, that's a bonus.

Place

Have you a special interest in, or knowledge of, a particular area, city, country? Again, this could be the starting point for your blockbuster, but try to approach your background with the wide-eyed curiosity of the newcomer – that way you'll write about it more vividly. We'll discuss research, its use and abuse, elsewhere, but for now remember that, like historical background, it's secondary to the characters and the story. Researched material can create atmosphere and colour but it cannot, on its own, persuade the reader to turn the page.

Milieu

Otherwise known as 'The world of . . . '. Obvious examples of this kind of blockbuster are Jilly Cooper's *Riders, Rivals* and *Polo*. More recently we've had Tim Geary's stylish and scurrilous bestseller about the world of male models, *Ego*. Most of Jackie Collins' novels come under this heading, as do Arthur Hailey's, and in the American bestseller list at the moment it seems to be raining lawyers. The milieu type of background has one great advantage – it presupposes a certain knowledge of the people involved, their motivation and preoccupations and what makes them tick. If you've worked in a place, and you're even averagely observant – as a writer you're probably nosey as hell – you'll have absorbed a priceless fund of information about your colleagues.

Theme

In the development of ideas we need to differentiate at an early stage between theme, story, and plot.

Theme is crucially important in the blockbuster. We're aiming for a huge book, epic in scale and panoramic in scope, but which can be summed up by Sophie Spritzer of *Marketing* in no more than a dozen simple words. In response to the question: 'What's it about?' you must be able to answer loud and clear: 'One woman's search for her true identity in Tsarist Russia', or 'Passion that transcends this century's bitterest conflict', or 'From barrow-boy to banker', or 'Revenge and romance in old Hong Kong'.

Your book's theme is its underlying impetus, its nature, its feel. It will have to do with emotion or motivation – jealousy, lust, loyalty, retribution, friendship, greed, loneliness, faith, ambition – with knobs on according to period, place and personal preference. The Search makes a wonderful theme – the search for fulfilment/happiness/identity/love/inner peace. The search denotes a personal journey of some kind, profoundly motivated, enduring and with built-in dramatic tension – will the object of the search be found?

When talking about the importance and significance of titles, I mentioned resonance. A strong, identifiable theme will give your book resonance and will inform the title. Take *Kane and Abel*. In those three words we have our theme – the deadly lifelong rivalry between two men. A strong theme will also be an absolute godsend both to the writer of your cover copy and your publisher's sales force, of whom more later.

It's often said that a writer's themes, in the sense of recurring features, 'emerge' – in other words that they are not planned or deliberate, but a product of the subconscious, surfacing at regular intervals. Critics take a certain pride in drawing attention to these, as though they had personally discovered some hitherto unrecognised aspect of the author's work, and it is true that many of us do have themes we aren't aware of until they're pointed out to us. I was several books along the road before someone told me that my novels often contained a crusty and eccentric father who has a love/hate relationship with his wilful daughter. It was perfectly true, but this particular scenario was not premeditated. Now of course I feel self-conscious and would go to some lengths to avoid repeating it, so a small element of spontaneity has been lost.

Births are another preoccupation of mine. For reasons buried deep in my psyche – I'm no mother-earth figure, as my children will testify – a birth figures prominently in many of my novels.

A third persistent thread is the dog – I can't seem to write a book without a dog in it. I'm not just talking unidentified peripheral dogs here, but fully-fledged characters with names, attributes, personal histories and a part to play in the unfolding story. The dog is both an individual and the familiar of its attendant human. This is a tendency I strive to curb, but it keeps getting the better of me. In my novel *Both Your Houses* I sidelined the obligatory dog by making it the pet of a secondary character, but the hole at the centre of the action was so obvious to me that in the end I introduced a recently-destroyed dog who was affecting his owners from, as it were, beyond the grave . . .

I digress: the point I'm trying to make is that this sort of personal preoccupation is wholly, if not always, unpremeditated.

But in the blockbuster, even if other lesser themes are left to emerge along the way, we must decide in advance on our underlying theme. A little craftiness in this regard early on may reap dividends later. The fact is that the great themes, some of which

I've mentioned, are universal. They ring true and strong whatever the background of your novel; only a reader of stone could fail to identify with them. And universality is what we're after. QED.

Don't, for goodness' sake, sit down at your desk with a list of themes, close your eyes and plant the ballpoint somewhere on the paper. We may not wish to leave our theme to chance, but neither do we wish to be saddled with it. As with so much to do with writing, you must play psychological games. As the original idea germinates and grows, as the characters flesh out and the background fills in, a theme will become apparent and you can ambush it. It may be something bold and brassy like 'Passion in check – forbidden love among the chess set', or more sophisticated: 'Your family you're born with – your friends you choose'. At any rate you will have begun to get a feel for the *essence* of the book.

Theme is especially important in the blockbuster because this has to be a book with real stage presence. A theme shows at once that the writer takes a large view, and that the story encompasses not just the specific characters and events it chronicles, but the whole human condition. Remember, the reader, or potential buyer browsing in a bookshop, doesn't know that you're a housewife from Upper Gumtree, the peak of whose social activity is being secretary of the Inner Wheel. Even quite famous novelists enjoy relative public anonymity, and you and I can rest easy in the knowledge that the mundane secrets of our private lives are perfectly safe. In print, we can afford to assume an altogether more imposing identity.

Hypothesise

Ask yourself 'What if . . . ?' Fly kites. Run a few notions up the flagpole and see if anyone salutes. A thought-provoking hypothesis can be the sole basis for a blockbuster – *The Eagle Has Landed, SSGB, The Day of the Jackal* – or it may simply provide you with a particular facet of your story which will add to its lustre. It will almost invariably take the form of a question. On the flyleaf of *An Imperfect Lady* I quote the opening lines of a poem by Robert Graves entitled 'A Slice of Wedding Cake'. If you haven't read the poem, I urge you to do so: it's short and brutally funny about the men that so many women fall for. I first heard it recited by Graves himself in a one-man show at the Mermaid Theatre in the early seventies. It went into the mental odd-sock drawer – until the day came when it presented itself as the perfect starting point. Why *do* some women persistently fall for the 'wrong' person? What is going on there? Are they nature's victims, or guilty only of loving 'not wisely but too well'? Is it a compulsion, a pattern, or random chance?

This question teamed up with another. It seemed to me that popular fiction is positively clogged with the 'He done her wrong' type of story, in which an innocent scullery maid, having been tampered with by the young master in her formative years, rises to become Chairperson of ICI, her sole motivation that of grinding men's faces into the dust. She most particularly wants to grind the face of the young master (which is pretty pointless because by this time he's got his bus pass and wouldn't say boo to a goose). It made for a good story, but *what if* one were to stand the whole thing on its head?

What if our heroine, far from being a scullery maid, is handsome, wealthy and talented? And what if, far from wanting to grind men's faces in the dust, she forms a whole series of passionate attachments to people who are simply not worthy of her but whom she loves to death? I liked the idea of this woman – as a feisty septuagenarian – looking back on her life at the end of the book with a smile on her lips and a song in her heart because the world had been well lost for love.

The why? and the what if? here came together to give me the initial idea, the story and the theme of *An Imperfect Lady*.

You'll notice that both these ideas arose, initially, from something I'd read, which brings me on to my next point.

Reading

I hate to be a nag, but you have *got* to read. Like most authors, I run creative writing workshops from time to time, and speak, when invited, to writers' circles and at summer schools, and I'm continually amazed at the number of would-be writers who scarcely read. For ideas to germinate and proliferate there has to be fertile ground to sow them in, and for the ground to be fertile it must be mulched with observation, imagination, and *other writing*.

Now please understand there is no question of your getting the ideas themselves from other novels. Second-hand is second-rate by definition, although there is some truth in the aphorism that there are only half a dozen basic storylines . . . You don't want to copy any other writer, quite the reverse, but in order to find out what kind of writer you are, you need to have read widely. Only exposure to a variety of different styles and approaches will help you find your own feet.

Read all the time – don't regard it as some sort of frivolous and degenerate activity which prevents you shampooing the carpet, filling in the tax return or detoxing the cat. That's old fashioned and unprofessional. It was our great-great-grandparents who spoke of a child 'always having her nose in a novel' rather as we might speak of the child whose hands are soldered to her Game Boy. It is part of your sacred duty as a writer to read, passionately and avidly.

Don't be too selective – pick up anything you think you might enjoy, and then add the same number you're not quite so sure about, and off you go. If anything really bores you or doesn't hold your attention when you've given it a fair go, discard it by all means, but not before you've at least attempted to discover where, for you, it failed. If one author particularly attracts you, get hold of her other novels. When you've finished something which held you enthralled for hours, then ask yourself why it worked? What was it that made it so compelling? What did the writer do? It won't be easy, but tussle with it. Now's the time to be analytical. The allure of a particular novel for us has a lot to do with what goes on in the writer's mind. Reading novels is a magical mystery tour around the inside of other people's heads. Taking that tour, just like going on holiday in real life, will make us appreciate our own place when we get back to it. We will see our strengths – and our weaknesses – and have a greater appreciation of what we can do to to enhance the first and play down the second.

Make sure you read other blockbusters. Not exclusively, but include some in there. After all, the mere fact that you've bought this book and are thinking of setting out to write a blockbuster should tell you that you are determined and professional, and therefore not above a little research. Don't just read – mark, learn and inwardly digest. Dissect and analyse. I'm not suggesting that you copy, but that you take a sensible approach to your craft, and then go away and get artistic . . .

What you need to do is establish the parameters within which you're going to operate. Any editor will tell you that for a first-time novelist, writing within a particular genre is the best bet. A blockbuster may not be a genre, but it has certain defining characteristics, some of which we've already covered. Your job is to meet all the criteria and then (hardest but most vital of all) to imbue the writing with your own inimitable, unique spark, the originality of thought and imagination which only you can bring to it. *That*'s what makes an editor's day. It's a juggling act, but you can do it.

Don't do it!

To close this section, I'm going to speak treason – if you think it might upset you, look away now.

The received wisdom goes: Write about what you know.

I implore you: Don't.

Aargh . . . ! I can sense the ripples of unease spreading through a thousand writers' circles, creative writing classes, novel seminars and fiction workshops. 'Write about what you know' is one of those sacred tenets of the writer's creed which has been passed around reverentially for so long that people have stopped thinking about it.

Think about it now. One of the criticisms most often levelled at first novels is that they're self-indulgent. And one of the reasons they tend to attract this particular criticism is that they're autobiographical. I have certainly written novels based on personal experience, but much further into my career, when I was more aware of how to use that experience in fictional form – and those novels were not blockbusters. It's always seemed to me to be curious and perverse to encourage first-time novelists to cannibalise their own lives in their writing, when a) the material may be dull as ditchwater and b) they are far too close to it to be able to fictionalise it successfully. If, as I said earlier, you know a particular place or milieu especially well and can make use of it in the context of your novel, fine, but remember that you must distance yourself from it, take it apart and then reconstruct it in a heightened version of itself. Some of us may lead, or have led, the sort of lives that are blockbuster material, but most of us don't. It takes an extraordinary talent to turn the humdrum and quotidian into a million-seller of the kind we're addressing here. It can be done, but I'd be failing in my duty if I suggested that it was your best course of action. That something is true does not necessarily make it riveting.

Emotional truth, though, does. And this is where the advice to 'write about what you know' – so often, and mistakenly, taken literally – comes into its own. You put your imagination to work on the characters, story, setting and plot . . . wherever possible you enliven them with observation culled from personal experience . . . and then you make sure that every nuance of character, every action sequence and piece of dialogue is informed by what you, as a well-rounded human being, have learned of the human condition. You may not know what it's like to confront a drug-crazed Triad gunman in a dark alley in Hong Kong's walled city, but you do know about fear, and anger, and the adrenalin-rush or frozen inertia that they induce. And because you have created fully formed characters you will know how they are likely to respond in this imagined situation.

Your blockbuster may be as far removed geographically and in period from your own life as it is possible to be, but it will pack power and carry conviction if it has emotional truth.

The novel is primarily a work of the imagination, given substance and reality by the author's understanding and perceptions. Become a student of human nature. It's not pretentious, it's common sense.

4

THE GRAND PLAN

My father, a military man, had a favourite saying: 'Time spent on reconnaissance is never wasted'. I think he was right. Almost anything you undertake is easier if you're well prepared. It comes naturally to me because I'm one of nature's list-makers. No day is complete without its accompanying scrap of paper, with its just-legible jottings of stuff to do, bits to buy, calls to make and letters to write, and this habit finds its apotheosis in the planning of a novel.

Must I?

There's no 'must' about it. There are plenty of writers (and I confess I rather envy them) who claim simply to pick up a blank sheet of paper and begin – following, as it were, whither the muse leads. Perhaps you know the famous Joyce Grenfell monologue, 'The Writer of Children's Books', of which the following is a sample:

> 'Hallo, boys and girls. I was so pleased when you asked me to come along and tell you how I write my books for children. Well, of course, the answer is – I don't. No, my books write themselves for me . . . First of all I go upstairs to my Hidey-Hole . . . I pin a notice on the door and it says: 'Gone to Make Believe Land' . . . I put a clean white sheet of paper in my typewriter and I sit down in front of it and I close my eyes . . . And I sit there and I type and type, and as I do so I learn all about Jennifer-Ann's unruly mop of red curls and her way with hedgehogs . . . Then all of a sudden it's dinner time and I find myself back in my Hidey-Hole – and look! – a great pile of typed pages on the table beside me. They must have written themselves while the story told itself to me . . .'

Wicked stuff! And the cleverest thing about it is the way Joyce Grenfell conveys that beneath all the guff about books 'writing themselves' is a steely professional with one eye on the market and another on her bank balance. Please understand, I'm not trying to imply that writers who say they don't plan are fibbers, or that all writers are hard-boiled cynics. But it's my entirely subjective and personal opinion that even people who don't plan on paper allow an idea to roll around in the subconscious long enough to have acquired a shape; nuances of character and plot; a taste or tone of its own; and very probably an arresting opening and ending, too. If the idea was good enough to begin with, the imaginative juices will have been getting to work on it.

The point is that no matter what the obvious degree of planning, a sound understanding and knowledge of your own idea will give your storytelling confidence, and confidence is especially important to the blockbuster. The reader must feel swept up, swept along and ultimately swept away by your narrative. This is not the type of book in which to abandon yourself completely to the whims and vagaries of random inspiration.

'Soft think'

I don't much care for buzz-words and jargon, but occasionally they come in useful as shorthand for a complicated idea which would otherwise be cumbersome to repeat. That's why I'm going to use the business-school terms 'soft think' and 'hard think'.

If you're an established writer, there is a pleasurable period after a book has been delivered during which you go for long walks, shop for clothes, see friends, cook the occasional dinner and kid yourself that you absolutely have to buzz into town to lunch with your agent/editor/old school chum. You can coast for a while on the fact that you have (with any luck) a book in the shops, another with the publisher, and a third 'taking shape' about which you are very excited. It's all terribly cosy and gratifying.

That third book, the one that still exists solely in your head, will have risen to the top of the mental box-room over the previous few months and you will have begun, if only subconsciously, to develop and embellish it. During the natural break following delivery and completion, more will happen. A contented, sitting-on-the-nest feeling will overcome you. You nurse and cherish the idea. It retains a perfect, shiny wholeness because it has not, as yet, been exposed to the harsh light and crunching pressures of reality.

If you're a first-time, or as-yet-unpublished novelist you may ironically feel more fired-up and keen to begin. This is because you've not yet experienced the jolt that accompanies the transition from expectation to execution. Those who have are adept at spinning out the soft-think stage. There is nothing in the way of inspirational music, deep discussion, peaceful thought and background reading that they will not undertake in the interests of postponing the evil hour. The temptations of unending research are well-known and will be set out in greater detail elsewhere.

At any rate, there comes a moment (and you will develop, I promise you, an inner voice that tells you when that moment is nigh) when you have to move things on.

Sells and blurbs

To ease your way into the next stage, try selling the book to yourself. My women's magazine training, distant though it is, gave me an appreciation of the 'sell' – that short paragraph in bold type, sometimes in the 'next week's box', sometimes sandwiched between the title and the main copy, which not only encapsulates what the piece is about but does its darnedest to make you want to read on. Later I encountered the ghastly form sent out by publishers to their new authors, and at regular though infrequent intervals thereafter, which asks for background both personal and professional, hobbies and activities, qualifications – and a description of your book as it might appear on the jacket. A blurb, in fact. This is usually a major stumbling block, especially for first-time authors who may feel acutely embarrassed at being asked to blow their own trumpet in this way, and in print, too! I can remember being convinced that if I made *The Flowers of the Field* sound too exciting, everyone at Futura would mark me down as bumptious and/or pretentious, and I would be universally shunned.

Here's what I wrote on the form:

> '*The Flowers of the Field* is set in the period of the Great War, and chronicles the lives and relationships of three women. The heroine, Thea, is ambitious, and becomes an ambulance driver on the Western Front. Her flighty younger sister, Dulcie, finds a less orthodox route to personal fulfilment. The family's maid, Primmy, breaks though social barriers to achieve independence in her work as a nurse. The lives of these three form the basis of a story which encompasses love, personal conflict and the radical changes brought about by war.'

Nothing the matter with it – it's truthful and competent. In contrast, here's part of what Futura wrote in their catalogue:

> '*The Flowers of the Field* – The story of three young women whose lives are irrevocably changed by love, ambition and war . . . Out of family division and world chaos comes a new generation of women. Their independent struggles for fulfilment as a new era unfolds are captured in the epic novel of our time . . . '

And on the back of the paperback:

> 'From London and the fields of Kent to Paris, Berlin and the Western Front, the lives of three very different women are changed irrevocably by love, ambition and the First World War . . . Dorothea, Dulcie and Primmy. Their dreams and aspirations found a voice above history's most horrifying conflict. Their triumphs and tragedies were shared by a generation. Their unforgettable story unfolds in the epic novel of our time.'

Well . . . You wouldn't expect the publisher to have written the first of these blurbs, nor the author to have written either of the second two. But if you can produce a paragraph which falls somewhere in between the two, and which really flies the flag for your idea and conveys your excitement about it, you'll be doing everyone a favour. The writing of an arresting sell is not only helpful for the publishers (who incidentally love bumptious, up-front authors), since they may be able to use it as a basis for their blurb, but a useful exercise for you, too.

34

So have a go. Try on one or two for size, and when you hit the one that seems right it will give you a buzz, it will ring true in your own ears. It's almost like trying on a hat. Your book must suit you, it must seem both an extension and an enhancement of your personality, it must feel totally 'you' – but you at your best.

Not for nothing, however, is it called a sell. Make sure you're setting out to write the blockbuster you, your best friend, your neighbour and the woman in the airport departure lounge would be most likely to pick off the shelf. Be honest – don't traduce yourself. Be mindful of my earlier warning not to write 'down' in any way. The sell is the bridge that links 'soft think' to –

'Hard think' – plot

By now you will already have your story in mind – roughly what the premise is, and the sequence of events. You'll have summed up its theme, its unique 'taste' in your sell. Now for the plot.

There is a difference between story and plot. The plot is strategy and tactics – the way you choose to deploy the various factors in your story. Lavish care on it. This, after all, is your unique storytelling technique. There may be only a finite number of storylines in the world but there are an infinite number of plots.

To use a nautical metaphor: spread out your chart, your 'given' information – your story – on the table before you and then plot your course. From London to Sydney may be a certain number of miles as the crow flies, and the swiftest and most direct method of getting there may be by plane, but the alternatives are legion according to what sort of experience you wish the journey to be:

- You may wish to miss some places altogether and linger in others.
- You may want to go via the Russian steppes.
- You may not want to start in London at all, but to begin your journey in, say, Singapore, then retrace your steps to London via Ethiopia and Rome, and then finally zoom to Sydney.
- You may wish to make the journey overland, by foot, and by sea.
- You may not wish to do the travelling yourself at all, but to watch someone else undertake it.

- You may wish deliberately to try, say, three different routes in order to compare and contrast them.
- Sydney may have been the destination you first had in mind, but on reflection you could decide to stop well short of it – or leapfrog it and go to New Zealand.

Now let's apply this analogy to the business of creating a plot. Here's a fairly simple story by way of example:

A middle-aged woman hears that her first husband, whom she divorced some years earlier, has died. Having married again, he leaves a widow in her twenties and three young children. The first wife contacts the widow and comes to visit, with her blessing. She goes to the chapel of rest to see the man who has died. When she looks in the coffin the body is not that of her former husband. She is deeply shocked, and doesn't know whether to tell the young widow or not. What she eventually discovers is that she's looking through the telescope from the wrong end – it was her husband who assumed this man's identity, not the other way round. Why? And if her ex-husband has not died, where is he now?

I'm not going to supply the denouement to this story because a) I haven't thought of it yet and b) I rather like the idea and may well use it some time. At any rate, there it is, the story-map spread out in front of us, and there's a whole list of questions you can now ask yourself:

- Whose story is it? For the sake of ease my short outline makes it the first wife's, but it doesn't have to be.
- When is it set?
- Where is it set?
- What's the time-frame, i.e. at what point in the sequence of events are you going to start?
- Where are you placing the emphasis – on the mystery? The relationships? The after-effects?
- Will you use first- or third-person narration? If first, will it always be the same 'I'?
- Could it be black comedy?
- Or the starting point for a huge family saga?

36

● Could the whole thing simply be a newspaper item read by an outsider, which sets off a different but tangentially connected chain of events?

It's the answers you give to these questions which will determine your plot.

You're in charge

Nowhere is it cast in concrete that you must follow a set pattern or do things in a particular way. The blockbuster is not a genre, but a class of novel. As long as you bear in mind that you are aiming at the widest possible audience and that therefore it might be unwise completely to renounce punctuation, capital letters and standard spelling, you can – indeed must – write your own rules. Ask any editor – what they most yearn for and greet with tears of joy when it comes along, is a mass-market novel with obvious broad appeal, but also bearing the unmistakable, inimitable stamp of its author – a popular success with individuality.

Analogous is the belief of many adults that school uniform is a good idea because it's a leveller. Everyone will be the same, insist uniform's advocates – no more decisions over what to wear, no odious comparisons between the rich and not-so-rich kids, because they will be like peas in a pod, a mass, mobile logo for the school's corporate ethos.

Junk, of course. Anyone who has ever worn school uniform will tell you that nothing throws individuals into sharper relief than putting them in the same clothes. The child's – and more especially the teenager's – ability to customise her attire should never be underestimated. Everything from hat-brims to hemlines is subject to her opportunist creativity. The garment does not exist which will not in the end yield to the ministrations of a really determined schoolgirl with subversion on her mind.

The same with your novel. Never be afraid to embark on a genre which has clear conventions and boundaries. Such a novel offers wonderful opportunities for the uniquely individual touch. It is not philistine but truthful to say that you are more likely to be remembered for your fresh and original interpretation of the romantic novel than for some experimental prose-poem set in seventeenth-century Tibet.

Plot your blockbuster with zest, and have dramatic impact always in mind. One editor told me that plotting a novel could in one respect be compared to composing an opera: each section, or chapter, should contain an aria, or key scene, which is the core of that section. Recitative – the bread and butter stuff, the mere relaying of the facts – is necessary, but is not what the audience is there for. Who'd want to go to an opera entirely made up of recitative? Your aria, or dramatic scene, is what your chapter leads up to or is built round. (When I use the term 'dramatic' I don't necessarily mean dramatic in the Bruce Willis sense – there need be 'no wrecks nor nobody drownded'. A scene of quiet intensity, or of sharp humour or elegiac sadness can be dramatic. The degree of drama will depend on how crucial it is to your story.)

In common with many other novelists, what I do is this:

- I get a single sheet of A4 paper.
- Down the left-hand side I put a column of double-spaced numbers, not fewer than twelve and not more than thirty – potential chapters.
- Against each number I write in not more than two or three lines what the chapter is about.
- Every chapter must either develop the characters or advance the action – preferably both.
- I avoid 'stretching' the outline beyond its natural limits.
- Any chapters which smack of padding, or treading water, I excise.

Plotting is all about setting up the narrative pull, and the inbuilt dramatic tensions which keep it taut. Keep your foot on the clutch – consider how much to tell the reader now, how much to keep up your sleeve for later. You're in charge. The greater your confidence, the greater the reader's. If you've ever been to an amateur drama production, you'll know how edgy it makes you when the scenery sways, or there are too many prompts. The illusion breaks down, and the hesitation and anxiety are all you notice. Same thing with the novel, especially the blockbuster.

Good, tight plotting creates narrative tension, which not only makes the book more gripping to read, but will be of considerable assistance to you, the author. Planning can't ensure that you never have a bad day – this is not cloud-cuckoo land – but it will help you maintain impetus and direction, and stay purposeful.

Surprise, surprise!

Excitement is a key factor in any kind of creative endeavour. When people talk of being 'inspired' they refer to a sense of intense excitement which carries them along and makes them impatient to put their ideas into practice before they evaporate. Other terms you hear used to describe this sensation are achieving 'flow' and being 'on a roll'. Keeping this excitement going during the writing process is one thing, and I'll offer a few thoughts on that later. But guarding against losing it at the start is essential. *Don't give too much away.*

Whether this is your first novel, or simply your first attempt to write a blockbuster, there will be polite pressure to pre-sell your idea to an agent and/or publisher. This makes sound business sense, and it would be irritatingly precious of you to refuse if pressed. On the other hand, you want to knock 'em dead, and the element of surprise will be an important factor in your success. So keep something back.

This, like many of the other really juicy nuggets of advice you come across here, will be repeated in just about any other 'How To' book on writing that you care to pick up. But it bears all the repetition because it's so true. Excitement and inspiration flourish in a hothouse. Open the door for too long and some of that precious heat is lost. Also, when you elaborate on an idea to someone else it ceases to be entirely your property, you quite literally give part of it away. Avoid this at all costs. Dennis Potter said that creativity thrives on repression. Hug your desires and aspirations to yourself, and let them flourish in private until you're ready to disclose them.

So you've captured that original, magical idea. You've set it down, given it a form, fleshed it out and presented it (to yourself) in a way which will enable you to make it your own, and to keep your focus. But there's one absolutely crucial ingredient we've not yet mentioned.

5

WHO'S IN IT?

Story, plot, theme, planning, attitude – all are nothing without good characters. Something I've found hard in writing this book is how to present separately and sequentially the elements of what is essentially a complex, interrelated, organic process. But what is certain is that you cannot at this stage set pen to paper or digit to keyboard without knowing, intimately, the people with whom you are destined to spend most of your waking life for the next year or so.

Characters – or a character – may or may not be the starting point of your story, but what's certain is that it is the characters, and more specifically their motivation, which make up the motor that drives the story. They are also an indispensable factor in the compulsive readability stakes – without which your book hasn't a prayer of becoming a blockbuster. After all, if the reader doesn't care about the characters or what happens to them, why on earth should she turn the page? If the characters are unbelievable, one-dimensional, or treated with contempt by the writer, then why should what happens to them be of any interest to the reader?

This is true of all fiction, but like every piece of received writing wisdom, it is by definition doubly true of the blockbuster. If your aim is nothing less than total success, you'd better get this stuff right.

I'd like to outline, in descending order of importance, what will make your characters powerful, credible, and riveting.

Motivation

We could call it Motor-vation.

Thinking of it like that acts as a useful reminder that the story and plot, no matter how much midnight oil you may have expended on them, must be propelled by the desires, fears and aspirations of your characters. Ask yourself what your main character wants. Not simply in material terms – a big house, a better job, a fast car – but what makes her tick, what drives her. She may well be fiercely ambitious, but in a blockbuster that ambition must be overweening, all-consuming, an unstoppable force that sweeps aside obstacles and relegates everything else to second place. In *Kane and Abel*, Jeffrey Archer uses the parallel ambitions of two men, connected by fate, as the thrust of his narrative. We the readers know that sooner or later these two will clash. The irresistible force will encounter the immovable object with cataclysmic results. This underlying drive and the thrilling inevitability of conflict between the protagonists keeps us glued to the page. It informs and enlivens all the other ramifications of plot and character.

The pitfall in creating strong motivation of this kind is that the character might turn out to be a) unsympathetic and b) not fully rounded. The answer to both problems is the same – you must know that character inside out. Know far more about her than ever appears on the page. Whether or not you actually make notes about her, have a clear sense of where she comes from, both literally and figuratively. What forces have worked on her to make her the way she is? What influences? Who were her parents? Her siblings? Where and how was she brought up? Where educated (if at all)? What has been her experience of human relationships? If she is a tough, thrusting character does she have a hidden weakness? If she is diffident, what will it take to spark her to anger or passion? Which aspects of herself is she anxious to display, and which to conceal?

How much of all this you reveal to the reader is entirely up to you. You're in the driving seat. But your complete understanding of the characters and the source of their motivation is essential to your story's emotional credibility.

A character motivated by pure material ambition is energetic and acquisitive – she wants something, and when she has that something in her grasp is not satisfied but immediately wants more. But motivation need not be as obvious as this. It can take the form of a particular personality type. Earlier I mentioned 'the search' as being a good theme; and the search for love is probably the strongest motivation of all, because it underpins so much else and is so widely experienced. Even a hard-nosed, egocentric business tycoon may be at bottom a frantic little boy still trying to gain the approval of a cold or distant parent.

Examples

In *An Imperfect Lady* my heroine, Adeline Farrell, is a woman with a fatal weakness for unsuitable partners. She loves not wisely but too well – over and over again – to the despair of her family and friends. This susceptibility is her motivation. In a book which charts her life from childhood to old age it is the single most dominating influence, the source of drama and tension, and it provides the story with an ending which is both poignant and uplifting, for here is a woman who at the end of her long, turbulent life, and in spite of much sadness, feels that she has won, not lost.

In *A Flower That's Free* I was faced with all the characteristic problems of the sequel – a sense of *déjà vu*, the need to continue with what had been in the first place a long saga, and the difficulty of following, in the same vein, a book which had been a thumping international success. Far from feeling liberated, energetic and optimistic I felt constrained and paralysed. What more was there to say about these characters? They had the advantage that I knew them well – but so did the reader. The three women at the heart of the story had, at the end of *The Flowers of the Field*, achieved their very different kinds of independence and fulfilment through the harrowing experience of the Great War. In the second book they were coming to terms with the reality of that fulfilment. What I needed was a new, younger central character whose fresh motivation would give this book a thrust all of its own.

When I found Kate Kingsley, the book finally took off. Kate's fierce struggle to be her own woman masks a contradictory impulse – the need to find her roots, and to learn to accept love from others. When she finds the first and learns the second, then and only then is she truly free to be herself and the mistress of her own fate. Kate comes across to other characters in the novel as self-sufficient and even rather hard, but we who know her know why, and we want happiness for her as much as she wants it for herself. So there is keen dramatic irony in watching her make her mistakes on the road to peace and maturity, and satisfaction when she finally makes her mature choice of life.

Here is another example of motivation, classic in every sense: in *Jane Eyre*, Jane too wants love, but not without mutual respect, and not at any price. She is passionate, but principled. The reader is never in any doubt that once Rochester's painful secret is out his chances of keeping Jane are slim. The reason she comes across as strong and sympathetic, rather than the prim killjoy she might so easily seem, is because we know her so well. The intimate, first-person portrait which Charlotte Brontë offers us ensures that we are enrolled on Jane's side. We know – though Jane herself is sparing with the details – about her unhappy childhood with the Reeds and at Lowood, and we know too the kind of person this has made her. She may be small, plain and reticent, but we know her true worth. We admire and are attracted to Rochester for intuiting what we already know. Jane's motivation is that in her emotional life she will never settle for second best.

Change

Which brings me on to change. Change happens.

A couple of years ago I attended a school reunion. I went along somewhat grudgingly as a favour to the friend who was organising it. I told myself that I didn't believe in such pointless, sentimental harking back to the past, and couldn't see what possible point there would be in hanging around drinking warm German wine with a bunch of people many of whom I hadn't seen for over twenty years and never had much time for in the first place. Which all goes to show how wrong you can be.

Admiring cries of "You haven't changed a *bit*!" rang round the room, but as soon as we began talking to each other we realised the opposite was true. Girls who had been put-upon little mice in the upper dorm at school were now surgeons and marketing directors. The tall and haughty star of tennis court and swimming pool was a careworn divorcee bringing up three stroppy children on a secretary's salary in a provincial market town. The pouting nymphet who'd come second in a 'Britain's Brigitte Bardot' competition was living with another woman. The spirited young actress whose portrayal of St Joan had made my heart beat faster was a school dinner lady. The gawky class frump was a model. The poised and exquisite head girl was two stone overweight and had a son on drugs. The swot was a barrister, glitteringly single and riotously rich.

Not one of them was the same, or had even turned out as one might have predicted. The characteristics which had made them what they were at school, and the experiences they'd had since, had helped to form what they were now. After the surprise came the recognition, and then the tentative renegotiation of relationships according to this new order.

Whatever your character's motivation, the challenges, achievements and setbacks she encounters will have wrought some change in her by the end. The change may be in her circumstances, her relationships, her personality or her behaviour. It may be in all four. The dramatic events and emotional upheavals through which your characters live will alter them for ever.

An actor, reading her part in a script for the first time, looks for a 'through line' – the development of her character during the whole course of the play. Identifying this through line is the first and crucial step towards full characterisation. So with your central characters – establish the clear through line, by asking the questions: What makes them tick? What do they want? What do they end up with? How have they changed?

Universality

A difficult one, this, because of course your characters need to be unique and unforgettable individuals (see next section). But in a blockbuster novel you mustn't be afraid to make them larger than life.

Maybe I could describe it as the difference between actors on television and those in films – movie stars. The technique required for both is essentially naturalistic. (I had a great-uncle, himself an actor of the grand old huff-and-puff school, who dismissed to-day's practitioners with the scornful words: 'These people don't act, they just *behave*.' He was right: a new generation, accustomed to the close and unforgiving scrutiny of the camera, have only to 'think' a feeling to convey it.) But there the similarity ends. Television is an intimate medium, which we approach on equal terms. We interact with it. Because we watch television at home we are at least nominally in charge – we can switch it on and off, we can talk over it, leave it while we make cups of tea or cook meals, we can knit, write, read or make love in front of it, and we can ignore it altogether. One of television's most successful strands is soap opera, itself an open-ended, on-going distillation of 'real life'.

The cinema, whatever its subject matter, is a very different experience. In the cinema you, the customer, have made a conscious decision to step out of the everyday world into a dark, womb-like, shared environment. When the lights go down and the film begins to roll you are not simply entertained but transported. Though my great-uncle's style of histrionic projection would still be ludicrous, the scale of the entertainment is overwhelming – the height and breadth of the screen, the intensity of light and colour, the volume of sound and the size of the images make a good film absolutely compelling and unforgettable. When we emerge into the real world it seems a drab, grey, passionless place because our heads are literally filled with what we have just seen.

There are movie stars who are also great actors (De Niro, Streep, Hackman, Malkovitch), but it's not a prerequisite. From Cary Grant to Jack Nicholson, from Katherine Hepburn to Julia Roberts, from Bogey and Edward G. to Arnie and Sly, what the huge stars have is the ability to *come across*. In their films they don't so much act as peddle versions of themselves, and they don't need to do more because their personalities are so well defined and so widely compelling that the whole world will watch them, enchanted. We idolise them because they seem to embody extravagant aspects of ourselves, or ourselves as we would like to be. The movie star with all her idiosyncrasies is more charming, more desirable, more witty, more courageous, more of a *mensch*, than we can ever be. It does not matter that we know so-and-so is so short he has to stand on a box to perform a clinch with his leading lady, or that someone

45

else wears hair extensions and is a lousy mother. These things may even help to make the illusion more powerful. Up there on the screen those people have a hotline to our emotions.

Think of the characters in your blockbuster as movie stars. Allow them to be big – to think apocalyptic thoughts, to take rash risks, to court danger and beauty, to fall headlong in love, and to hate with terrible single-mindedness. If they make mistakes, let them make them on a grand scale, and find redemption by the hard road. And endow them with the powerful physical and emotional allure of the screen gods and goddesses. Not perfection, which is the biggest turn-off going, but the larger-than-life presence, the emotional capacity and sensual authority of a Garbo or a Paul Newman.

Identity

That said, and having come over all unnecessary in the process, it's time I adjusted my dress, and my focus. I said perfection was a turn-off, and it is, because nobody's perfect, and any fictional character who is will be unbelievable, one-dimensional and completely unsympathetic. The great stars always have a flaw or a weakness – that makes them human, and that makes us love them. Arguably the greatest star of all, Marilyn Monroe, was also the most patently vulnerable, and she was adored by men and women alike. Reader-identification is crucially important. Your task in the blockbuster is to swoop and fly, but carry the reader with you, like Peter Pan taking Wendy by the hand and soaring through the nursery window and into the night sky. Don't let go of the reader's hand or you'll lose her sympathy and with it her interest.

Your main characters must be complete, complex individuals, with a full hand of quirks, faults, fears, obsessions, weaknesses and strengths. I specify main characters, because it's heroes and heroines who are hardest to handle in this respect. Peripheral characters often seem to spring fully armed from the imagination because they do not need that movie-star quality to the same degree. They can simply *be*. They don't have to carry the great narrative burden of the main protagonists. This is why so many writers of big novels feel tempted to spend time paddling around in the murky shallows of the sub-plot instead of breasting the huge waves and turbulent currents of the open sea – the story.

All that stuff about the devil having the best tunes is true, so it may help to give your main character a bit of the devil. Scarlett O'Hara is a minx, and a much more plausible and compelling heroine as a result. She enrages but captivates us, just as she enrages but captivates Rhett Butler. It's no surprise that Angélique and Amber are ladies with tempers – the proud beauty has the advantage over the submissive saint every time. In the biblical blockbuster *The Robe*, the hero Marcellus carries with him the burden of having been one of the Roman soldiers present at the Crucifixion – the soldier, in fact, who diced for Christ's robe, and won. The story chronicles Marcellus' discovery of love, and of belief, and his subsequent Christian martyrdom – and not a dry eye in the house.

Casting against the role

To revert to the acting metaphor for a moment, try 'casting against the role'. In other words, don't fall into stereotypes. Give a vicar a roving eye; make an assassin a committed Christian; the schoolmaster a rock singer. It's often the edges of people's personalities that make them interesting, and make them run.

In *An Imperfect Lady* I inverted one of the best-loved conventions of popular fiction – rags to riches. You know the one – a penniless teenage scullery-maid is going about her scullery-duties in a big house in turn-of-the-century Cornwall, when who should come in but the young master, flushed from the hunt . . . After a little preliminary tapping of the ivory crop against the mud-spattered riding boot, he makes his move, and our blameless young heroine suffers some unmentionable (though easily guessed-at) indignity at his hands. In retrospect, though, it's the making of her, because so fired up is she by this caddish treatment that in due course she rises to become chairperson of a multinational corporation, tearing around the globe in a Lear jet and whirling from bedroom to boardroom and back again like a thing possessed.

Which, of course, she is – possessed by the need for revenge on the young master and her consequent loathing of all men.

All this is excellent stuff. There's a theme, a search, a powerful, highly motivated heroine, a 'rise to fame' story covering many years, and a complex, satisfying plot. You won't have to be a genius to have guessed that I'm referring to *A Woman of Substance* by Barbara Taylor Bradford, one of the archetypal blockbusters of recent times.

I turned the scenario upside down and created Adeline Farrell, a woman with every advantage, but also the fatal weakness I described earlier – she lavishes her love on a series of unsuitable and unworthy people. What Adeline had going for her as a heroine was tremendous likeability – hers was a weakness that I fancy a great many people can sympathise with, or recognise in themselves. She's a warm, strong, passionate woman, but a poor judge of character. The reader, like Adeline's fictional family, must keep on forgiving her for her awful mistakes and the emotional damage she inflicts on herself. This puts the reader at a slight advantage, in itself no bad thing.

The Flowers of the Field has three heroines, one of whom, Thea Tennant, is the central figure and touchstone of the novel. As a character the odds are loaded against her. She is a nice – even a good – energetic, principled young woman. She carries the narrative burden. There was always a chance that she might come across as no more than a goody-two-shoes. What saves Thea from this awful fate is the presence of the other two women – her flighty, unscrupulous younger sister Dulcie, and the family's maid, Primmie Dilkes, a tough, working-class realist. With these two as foils and counterbalances Thea's character has a chance to show its mettle in confrontation and argument. She *can* bite back. At the end of the book Thea is a stronger, calmer person than she was to start with.

So faults, weaknesses and 'casting against the role' are all important in giving your character identity. Let's look now at identifying marks – the aspects of a character which make her 'visible' – a recognisable individual whom the reader would know instantly in the street. They can be summarised something like this:

- Appearance.
- Name.
- Props.
- Mannerisms.
- Relationships.

Appearance

We have to be able to visualise a character before we can wholly believe in her. I won't say that, as in life, appearance forms our first impression, because in a novel this is not necessarily the case. In fact you should resist the urge to describe someone fully the moment they appear unless there is a sound dramatic reason for so doing (for instance, if you have built up certain expectations in the minds of other characters as to how that person will look – or if there is something so extraordinary in the person's appearance that to be unaware of it would deprive the reader). Dispense telling details sparingly. Remember that it may be more useful to tell your reader that Alexander has a faint harelip scar than that he has blue eyes; and more interesting to say that Rosemary has a half-grown-out perm than that her hair is red. Avoid the kind of flat, overall description which the police routinely issue, unless that is the effect you specifically want to achieve.

You might consider presenting a character's appearance through the eyes of someone else at a particular point in the story. In the case of your hero or heroine, it's best if this is a reasonably sympathetic view because this is someone you want your reader to root for through several hundred pages. But this doesn't mean it has to be through rose-tinted spectacles.

Here's a description of a young woman:

> 'Victoria was small and slim. She had a pale, heart-shaped face with wide-set grey eyes and a straight nose above full lips. She wore no make-up or jewellery and her dark hair was tied smoothly back. Her suit was plain and well tailored, her shoes had only a low heel and her nails were cut short and unpolished. She was too sober-looking to be pretty but there was something quietly attractive about her.'

49

There's absolutely nothing the matter with this description of Victoria, just as there's absolutely nothing the matter with Victoria herself. It gives us plenty of information – but very little food for thought, little to get the imaginative juices flowing. And there's something peculiarly deadening about that 'there was something quietly attractive about her'. Says who? The writer, presumably. It would be more effective if the writer indicated this quality of Victoria's by other means (the difference between show and tell – more later).

Here's another version:

> 'Gabrielle followed his gaze and saw Victoria. Good God – *this* was her rival, the woman she'd come to fear? This small, plain, painfully neat person with her hair scraped back and her serviceable suit and her sensible, well-polished shoes? This unremarkable little body with unplucked eyebrows, who was currently turning her unadorned face upward to be kissed by the richest man in the room . . .'

More interesting, perhaps?

Of course this is an invidious exercise because Victoria – and Gabrielle – are off the top of my head and come to the page without any accompanying narrative context. I use the two examples simply to show different ways of doing things. One is not necessarily better than the other, but the second tends to be more vivid and engaging, because the description of one character not only becomes part of the story itself, but also helps to define the character of the person expressing this viewpoint.

The first description (without its final sentence) would be effective if it were used as a kind of trump card. Suppose everyone, including the reader, knew Victoria only by name as the powerful mistress of a millionaire. Sure of her position in his life, she rarely appears in public – then, at a glittering party to celebrate his sixtieth birthday, she arrives unannounced. It's not only her presence that is unexpected. Her appearance is the polar opposite of what everyone has imagined. As she appears framed in the doorway we are given a quiet, factual run-down on how she looks – a *coup de théâtre.*

50

Here's a third perspective on our heroine:

> 'He stared, but not only from curiosity. She was the most powerful woman in the room and she demonstrated it by her refusal to accept the conventions of the occasion. Amongst the couture clothes and big hair, the show-off jewellery and expensively honed bodies, her quiet appearance shrieked for attention. And besides, Guy, accustomed to notice such things, took in a short, deeply grooved upper lip, an arrogantly unblinking gaze, slender ankles and, beneath that school-teacher's suit, a lissome waist and a bosom to die for – probably, he thought (and felt himself harden), clothed in snow-white cotton underwear . . .'

So Guy's turned on by Victoria, and sees her understated outfit as a deliberately provocative statement. This puts into perspective Gabrielle's scornful incredulity. Now we've learned a good deal about Victoria, and Guy, and Gabrielle, simply from describing Victoria's appearance in a certain way. And remember that if Victoria is our heroine, we will probably already have received some idea of how she sees *herself* and why she affects the style (or lack of style) that she does. There's a lot of drama to be derived from the difference between how a character sees herself and how others see her. And it's a device which is pleasing to the reader because only she has access to both points of view. So remember:

- Not immediately.
- Not all at once.
- Telling details rather than a catalogue of information.
- Different perspectives.

Names

It's terribly important to get them right. They should be right not just for the character – her period, social class and background – but for the reader, too. In other words no matter how unusual they are they must be 'pronounceable' in the reader's mind. A glitch in that otherwise wonderful Anne Tyler novel *The Accidental Tour-*

ist is the christian name of the hero – Macon. Now, I asked myself, is that 'a' long or short? Is the 'c' soft or hard? Is that Macon as in Bacon? Or Macon as in Bracken? Or is it Macon as in Hasten? Or Macon as in 'Gas on'? You see the problem? Not a big one in the great scheme of things but enough to interfere slightly with my smooth reading of the story.

A few years ago I began a huge (potentially blockbuster) novel, much of which was set in Hungary. I abandoned it for a number of reasons, though it's not impossible I may go back to it some day. A minor stumbling block – though not the reason for abandoning it – was the problem of all those Hungarian names. Hungarian is so utterly different from English, its pronunciation and spelling so fiercely foreign, that it was hard finding names for the characters which would not constantly cause the reader to peck and stumble. Whole groups of contiguous consonants don't make for easy reading.

Similarly, names that end in 's' can be awkward in the plural or when used possessively. If someone's called Piers are you going to say 'Piers'' or 'Piers's'? I personally prefer the second, but plenty of people find that an irritation. In *An Imperfect Lady,* Adeline's landlady in London is called Mrs Fairyhouse. When referring to anything belonging to her I had to write 'Mrs Fairyhouse's', which is cumbersome, and the married couple 'the Fairyhouses' which is even worse. I felt I should have been calling them the 'Fairyhice'. I was wedded to the name and stuck with it regardless, but I'm sure it must have irritated readers.

Freshness and originality in names is desirable, but don't strain after it to the point where the veins stand out and your characters sound bizarre. Always bear in mind what names are likely under the circumstances. If your central character is the son of an eccentric Edwardian don then he may well be called Aloysius, Tertius, Hector or Mortmain. But if he's the child of an unemployed Tyneside dockworker in the 1930s any of those are pretty unlikely and Frank, Jack, Tom or Bob might be a better selection.

And then there's fashion. The same docker's son today might be called Jason, Sean, Carl or Derek. I suggest that there were few, if any, Kylies in the nineteenth century, and that Ethel and Norah were once glamorous names without the 'comedy-turn' ring that they have now (although of course one has to bear in mind the preconceptions of a modern audience).

Surnames are subject to pretty much the same rules, and change less, although if you're going far back in history they may have Gallicised or otherwise different spellings. Again, remember that French-sounding or double-barrelled surnames tend to be the property of the upper class.

Nicknames, abbreviations and diminutives are useful because they help to denote the difference in relationships between characters, and changes in mood – someone usually referred to as 'Chris' knows she's in the doghouse or about to be the recipient of bad news if she hears herself called 'Christine'. They can also be a cover for a character's embarrassment or anxiety about her real name, or an indication of some failing in the past which she prefers to keep hidden, about which only someone from the past would know.

A consideration for the blockbuster-writer is that some names just won't do. My grandmother had an incredibly dashing brother named Keith. In old family albums there's Keith, all sardonic smile and merry eyes, a romantic hero to his fingertips and the tragic victim of an early death in the Great War. But when I tried naming the central character in a novel Keith, my agent nearly had a seizure. 'You can't call a hero Keith!' she cried (and here I apologise to all Keiths), 'Keiths eat fish paste sandwiches and wear socks with sandals and Acrilan slacks and have very straight partings! Don't do it!' I didn't.

Props

By this I mean all kinds of external accessories which you may choose to give your character. I've mentioned my own predilection for dogs, but things like clothes, cars, music, pictures, books (or lack of them) can all speak volumes about the characters you create. Remember Ralph de Bricassart's shorts? And Princess Daisy's lurcher? And Bill Sykes' bull terrier? (damn, dogs again). The possessions people acquire are not only personal preferences, but signals sent out to the rest of the world. Not just 'this is what

I like' but 'I'm the kind of person who likes this'. Even the least pretentious person knows she is saying something about herself every time she puts on certain clothes or reads a particular newspaper. You can do the same for your characters.

Mannerisms

In a way they should come under 'Props' too, because the two are closely connected. Little behavioural quirks help fix the character in the reader's mind just as much as, if not more than, physical appearance. And they have the incomparable advantage of being *active* – they *show* the person in action. If we read of an elderly lady shakily pouring Lapsang tea into a Royal Doulton saucer, blowing on it and placing it on the carpet for her pet chihuahua, we learn more about that lady than if we are simply told that she dotes on her pet. The image is vivid and alive.

But beware. Don't underestimate the reader and overdo the mannerisms. It is enough to mention a mannerism once, and show it a couple of times – your reader isn't daft and will have hoisted it in.

That goes even more for anything on a larger scale. By all means give your heroine an irrational phobia about needles (such a phobia could be pivotal if she's up the Amazon without a paddle when cholera breaks out), but don't give in to the compulsion to keep on mentioning it in case the reader forgets. Call to mind how you assimilate information when you read a novel – easily, is the answer, and almost subliminally. You file it away as you read, and summon it up when needed, it's not even a conscious process. As a rule of thumb, stick to one good dramatic demonstration of the phobia (or obsession, or passion, or irrational dislike), one glancing reference much later on, and then the final calling into play. And you had better call it into play, otherwise the whole darn thing's a waste of space.

Relationships

This is probably the most telling way of displaying character. Just as we only know blue from green and red from yellow by seeing them together, and just as we recognise a tune from the relationship of one note to another, so we understand characters best when we see them interacting. Action and dialogue are the stuff of drama and of character – but I'm going to deal with dialogue in a later chapter.

Remember the different perspectives I used to describe a character's appearance a few pages back? That use of different perspectives will help flesh out your central character in every department. The quality which is irresistible to one person will be anathema to another and go completely unnoticed by a third. For instance, our heroine Victoria, seen (and heard) interacting with her powerful lover, with the speculative Guy and with the sceptical Gabrielle, will be perceived in three different lights (strong and alluring; sexy and manipulative; prim and schoomarmish, in that order); but only you the writer, and your reader, will have the complete picture.

In *A Flower That's Free,* the heroine Kate Kingsley falls in love with two men: Bill Maguire, a tough, worldly journalist; and Lawrence, an idealistic young officer. Through these two intense relationships, both of which last throughout the book, and between which she has ultimately to choose, we see the different sides of Kate. With Bill she is passionate, self-centred, wilful and amoral; with Lawrence gentler, more thoughtful, more stable and loving. As Kate changes, the dynamics of these relationships change. Her final choice marks a great step forward in her character. Here is the scene where, as a tough-minded but unsophisticated girl, she first meets Bill, in a grand Berlin Hotel on the eve of the 1936 Olympics:

'This is my niece, Kate Kingsley,' said Aubrey, with a trace of pride, 'and my nephew, Joe.'

'Charmed!' said Marty. They all shook hands. The girl had a direct, appraising stare and a commanding handshake.

'Congratulations on your cartwheel,' said Bill.

'I thought it was you,' was her reply. In her rather pale, set face her eyes were yellow bright, like windows into a lighted room. Bill retained her cool hand for a moment so that he and she remained standing while the others sat. 'You stole the show, you realize.'

'Good gracious' – she removed her hand with unembarassed firmness

– 'I certainly didn't mean to do that.'

He was amused by something incongruously tight-arsed in her tone, but as they sat down she gave him the hint of a smile, eyes narrowed. Bill swallowed his drink, and stared at her with undisguised interest. In spite of the affected primness of her opening remark, he could readily picture being in bed with her, and perhaps his thought was apparent, for he detected a slight snub, now, in the way she lifted her chin and turned her head to join in the conversation. Bill enjoyed the snub, too.

'You two have met already?' enquired Marty of Kate.

'I wouldn't say that.' Sharp and fresh as a lemon.

'I was merely and admiring onlooker,' put in Bill affably, knowing it would annoy her.

'Could I have a drink?' she asked, looking round imperiously.

'Why, my dear young lady!' Bill watched delightedly as Marty, all gallant apology now, snapped his fingers to attract the waiter and ordered lemonade for Joe and dry sherry for Kate, and the same again for the rest of them. Furnished with another drink, Bill conceived a plan and proceeded at once to put it into action. He leaned forward and addressed Aubrey.

'You know, if you would like to go anywhere in particular, I'd be very glad to help out. I do know this town.'

'That's awfully good of you!' Aubrey, as Bill had recognized, was flush with the success of the arrangements so far. 'Of course we shall be at the stadium tomorrow, for the opening ceremony, and after that –'

'What about tonight?' asked Bill. 'Any plans for this evening?'

'Now then, Bill!' Threateningly jocular, Marty turned away from his discussion with Ralph, thereby revealing that he had not been attending to what the old man was saying. 'Don't you go leading these good people astray!'

Bill shrugged ingenuously, as if to say, what, me? But in Aubrey he had a willing subject, and one who did not care to be patronized.

'We haven' arranged a thing,' said Aubrey firmly. 'But I must say it would be rather pleasant – why not?' He glanced at Kate who in turn stared levelly at Bill over the rim of her glass.

'It looks as though we're in your hands,' she said rather acidly.

'Splendid. Dinner and a club, then. I'll be here at eight.'

'Hm.' Marty sounded uneasy. 'And the best of British.' He rose from his chair like a great florid cactus. 'I think we'd better get along to lunch and leave these people in peace,' he said in a tone of one removing a disobedient child. He paused beside Kate, one hand on her shoulder. 'I'm only sorry to be going just when an attractive lady's arrived, but that's the story of my life.' Bill thought it was a pity Marty couldn't see Kate's face, which was a study in frosty distaste.

'See you tonight, then.'

They shook hands and departed. From across the room Bill glanced back at the family group in time to see Kate idly lift his own empty glass, sniff it curiously, and set it down again. This, like other things about her, made him smile.

At lunch, over the menu, Marty remarked: 'That girl, what an oddity!'

'You thought so?'

'Bony and rigid like a hockey stick.'

'Ah, but you noticed her.'

"I could hardly avoid it, now, could I?'

'I thought she was attractive. Unusually so.'

Relationships are mirrors, throwing back different aspects of the person reflected.

6

ER – WHERE ARE WE?

In giving advice one should never ignore the obvious, so I won't. The thing to remember about the background is – it's at the back.

The function of the setting in a novel is to provide a rich, authentic, fertile soil in which the characters and their story can bloom and grow. If you'd just planted several potentially gorgeous flowering shrubs in a border and they were looking a bit sad, you'd dig some stuff in around the roots and feed them at source. You wouldn't, I hope, come along and simply dump lorryloads of peat and fertiliser on top, swamping the lot.

Extraneous and unassimilated researched material is the besetting curse of the blockbuster-writer. This is because the background *is* important in a blockbuster. One of the charms of a big book is that it takes you into another world, probably one that up till now you've only gazed at from a distance. You mustn't short-change or cheat readers by promising a panorama and then affording them only a wretched glimpse (remember my strictures in an earlier chapter as to half-heartedness). Your job is to unfurl the rich tapestry, cover the huge canvas, and all that stuff, while not losing sight of the purpose of it all – to illuminate your particular story.

There are essentially three approaches to research. Either you know a huge amount about a given area, in which case you can afford to be sparing with the details because your writing will naturally carry authority. *Or* you have done loads of research and found out a lot, in which case the temptation will be to earn brownie points by putting too much in. *Or* you can be trading on the very little you know, putting it all in and hoping to kid the readers that there's piles more you're holding back. The stark reality is that most novelists belong to one of the second two groups, and of the two options the first is the safer. If you've read up extensively on the

Indian Mutiny and yearn to pass on what you've learned, you may risk boring the reader; but if you only know six facts about it and artfully deploy them to create an illusion of knowledge, unless you are very skilful you risk being rumbled, and losing the reader altogether. So let's assume that you are at least going to pay the book-buying public the compliment of doing your homework.

To assist in getting it right, there are three questions you should ask yourself. Why? What? and How?

Why?

Why have you chosen a particular background in the first place? We touched on this in an earlier chapter about ideas. You may be in the happy position of being able to answer: 'Because I'm the greatest living expert on twelfth century Mongolia/cardio-vascular surgery/Chief Sitting Bull/international chess/Nell Gwynne/ life below decks in the age of sail. In which case, bully for you. Interestingly, the experts don't usually suffer from the compulsion to tell all. Where information has been fully assimilated and digested over a period of time, the writer can simply imbue her writing with what she knows. She can instinctively differentiate between the precious metal and the dross, and assess what material can usefully be employed in the service of her story. Whether she's any good as a storyteller is a separate issue, not up for discussion here. So if you are lucky enough to be an expert on a place (Russia), period (Tsarist Russia) or milieu (court circles in Tsarist Russia) suitable for blockbusting, you're incredibly fortunate and probably don't need to read much of what follows.

For the rest of us, choices have to be made. First of all, let's clear some of the obvious no-no's out of the way. I've already taken my don't-write-what-you-know hobbyhorse out for a canter, but perhaps I could do a quick lap of honour. It's very unlikely you'll be able to forge a genuine blockbuster, in the terms of this book, out of goings-on on the local PTA, the cut-throat world of guineapig-showing, or mushroom culture in East Anglia. A gifted writer can make a compelling novel out of just about anything, but none of these scenarios, handled by the majority of us, has what it takes to be a humungous, world-wide, mega-selling hit. No, what we all know best is the human condition – emotions, situations, confrontations, passions – and *that* is what we should make use of in our writing.

So as to background, may I make a suggestion? Don't be cold-blooded about it. Go for something which attracts you, which has already engaged your interest, where perhaps there is some connection which will help bring it to life for you. Now I bet your heart's sinking. 'But I don't have any special interest in anything!' I hear you cry. It's like being asked what your hobbies are – suddenly you don't have any; or being stopped by the police – suddenly you're guilty. Just hang on. I'm not talking sensible here – I'm talking *chemistry*.

An example

Ages ago I went to see that film *The Charge of the Light Brigade*, with a starry cast including David Hemmings and Trevor Howard. I believe it was directed by Tony Richardson. Two contrasting images made an unforgettable impression on me. The first was a scene depicting the English troops leaving for the war – a scene of proudly billowing banners, brilliant uniforms, sparkling sea, stirring band music and lovely girls fluttering lace hankies. All was hope and heart and high spirits, perfectly caught in cinematic terms.

The following scene showed the same troops shortly after their arrival in the Crimea. Gone were the 'choice-cull'd chevaliers' who'd left England a few months before, and in their place trudged a tattered, travel-stained, heartsick column of shuffling conscripts – ill-fed, ill-prepared and just plain ill, oppressed by disease and stifling heat in an unknown land. Even the officers' horses hung their heads. Dirt and sweat had dulled the colourful uniforms and fear and poor diet had debilitated the men inside them. A sickly yellow sun stood in a feverish pale sky. A smog of dust hung about the column. And instead of band music, the sonorous buzzing of battalions of flies accompanied these men on their way to one of history's most scandalous humiliations . . .

It was the sound of those flies that did it. The hair rose on the back of my neck then, and it still does today as I tell you about it. That scene would be near the top in my ten favourite film moments. And it left me with a real desire to write, some day, a novel set in the Crimea.

The other hook which got me was an item on BBC Radio Two one afternoon a few years ago. I'm addicted to radio, and have it on all the time when I'm not working. On this occasion I was ploughing through an Everest of ironing when I heard an English army officer talking about the forthcoming rebuilding of the Sebastopol Memorial. He had one of those arresting patrician voices that stood out in what was an otherwise bland sea of mid-Atlantic classlessness. You could tell he wasn't used to being behind the microphone and in a strange sort of way his stiffness gave his remarks an authority that a more relaxed and professional presentation might have lacked. What he had to say was quite simple and didn't take long. He was launching a fund-raising drive to contribute to the new memorial. It was a very costly business, although the work was being done by Russian labour relatively cheaply. And all the surrounding land, he added, hundreds of acres of it, where thousands of British soldiers lay in unmarked graves, was going to be landscaped, and the dead properly honoured. I was reminded all over again of those men and horses with heads lowered in the heat, and the flies buzzing greedily around them.

It's not much to go on. And factually speaking I'm as pig-ignorant now as I was then. What I know about the period can still be summed up as: the Charge of the Light Brigade, the Lady with the Lamp, and attendant cardigans, wellingtons, and sandwiches. (How ironic, incidentally, that this shameful and bloody débâcle should be for ever associated with the three fundamental prerequisites for an English picnic.) But when I get round to my Crimea novel – which I definitely will – I shall approach the research with a real sense of excitement and anticipation, and all because of a scene in a film and a five-minute radio interview.

Alternatively, you might have some family association with a particular place or period. Did you have some eccentric, travel-stained old uncle who told stories about coffee-planting in Kenya at the time of Mau-Mau? Or are there any entertainers in the family (preferably ones who remember vaudeville, or who have done shows in Las Vegas)? Or what about fighter pilots . . . doctors . . . an upbringing in India? It doesn't have to be your own experience, just something you've listened to which caught your imagination at the time. What about that television series about Poland? Or that little item on the radio about reincarnation? Or your schoolgirl fascination with John of Gaunt? All or any of these could be the seed-corn which gets you started on research in the right frame of mind – fired-up, imagination racing, keen to tell your story.

Don't imagine that it will work to look at the current bestseller list either here, or on the other side of the Atlantic, or both, and use that to divine what background sells. I *could* tell you that historical novels aren't doing well just now (which, as I write, they're not), that they're out of fashion and out of favour and you'd do best to steer clear of them, but it would be most unwise of me to do so. Allowing for the time this slim volume will take in production, and then for the time it will take you to get round to reading it, and then begin writing your novel, the whole fiction fashion-cycle will have moved on and historicals could be hot once again. And anyway, if the story's terrific and you tell it as wonderfully as I know you can, the background will seem quite perfect, whatever it is. So be guided in this as in all things, gentle reader, by your heart – you'll be a more convincing writer for it.

What?

Having selected your background, how do you choose which bits to mug up on?

For starters, don't select too early. Picture the research process as a kind of pyramid – start with the broadest possible base and gradually home in on the intriguing, unusual and relevant bits.

If it's a historical background, I usually start by reading some absolutely basic (e.g. school textbook) kind of material on the period. Overview is the name of the game at this stage (my history is woefully inadequate), and all I'm trying to achieve is a sense of when things happened, their general historical context, who was ruling the relevant countries and with what degree of success and popularity. Now, given that I have an initial interest in the period for whatever reason, certain dates and events will spring off the page clamouring to be recognised. 'Ah, so that's when that was', you find yourself thinking. This is the stage at which you will begin to get a feel of how your imagined characters, story, theme and plot may dovetail with historical events as smoothly and seamlessly as tongue-and-groove flooring. Particular historical events may present themselves as the perfect occasion of sin – or love, or confrontation – and therefore more significant in terms of your story, which in turn allows others to drop into the background. The outbreak of war is always going to send ripples through the social fabric of any nation, and that will include your characters. Devastating battles, with their accompanying loss of life and the implications for those left behind, are the same. Don't be afraid to capitalise on the great events of history, but remember it's not your job to catalogue your view or anyone else's on the causes, conduct and effects of these events, but to imagine *what it must have been like to be there*. So get the details straight in your mind and then set them aside.

The initial overview will enable you to choose which areas and events to look into more thoroughly. Here again, start with basic information and then move on to the more anecdotal material – memoirs, diaries, newspaper cuttings. If the time you're writing about is in this century, then you can do no better than to try to talk to people who were alive then, and can remember. The highly selective but vivid memories of the old are more precious than rubies. It's as if a particular experience has been kept suspended in negative form, so it can be instantly re-processed again and again as fresh and crisp and bright as it was at the time.

Anyone can go and look up a matter of objective fact – like a date, or a place name, or a series of statistics – in a book. But not everyone can convey convincingly what it must have been like to be a pot-boy in Napoleon's army or a lady's maid to Mary Queen of Scots. You, through your talent and imagination assisted by discriminating research, can do that. Seek out the rare and valuable nuggets of firsthand experience like a pig snouting for truffles.

Don't be afraid to make things up, either. Making up incidents from an informed position is very different from fabricating them from a standing start because there's nothing else there. As you conduct your researches you'll begin to get the feel of the period, and what the possibilities and limitations are. You could take some glancing reference, no more than a gleam of a happening, and let your imagination work on it and fashion it into something both dramatic and historically plausible.

An example

When I was researching the background to *The Flowers of the Field* I spent a good deal of time in the Imperial War Museum's department of oral records (highly recommended). I listened to a lot of tapes. A woman who had been a nurse on the Western Front mentioned that one of her more harrowing tasks had been to remove personal possessions and valuables from the bodies of the dead, which often included German as well as English soldiers. She was a practical-sounding woman, who nonetheless recalled that to see the dead men, most of them still in or barely out of their teens, was to be reminded in the most devastating way that everyone was somebody's son. This isn't an astonishing or original *aperçu* in itself, but to hear her saying it in her rather dry and halting way was to know it afresh, and to imagine just what it must have been like for a twenty-year-old girl to pick over the corpses of boys no older and often even younger than herself, to uncover their most precious personal treasures and mementoes, to feel their cold, discoloured skin and to face the brutally shocking truth that, for them, life was over when it had scarcely begun.

The simple human drama of this scenario begged to be written into my story – for what if a young English nurse were to find the body of a German officer with whom she had fallen in love before the war? And what if he had on him a keepsake (in this case a tie-pin) given to him by someone she knew, during the fraternisation in No Man's Land at Christmas 1914? The setting would have complete authenticity, and the discovery would provide a tragic conclusion to the theme of the beloved enemy, and a symbol of hope for the future of another relationship...

Don't be afraid to use settings or material which may already be familiar to your readers. Newness and originality are to be commended, but don't underestimate the dramatic effect of treating familiar material in a fresh way. We like to read about some place, situation or historical event of which we have some knowledge, if only because it's easier to imagine. What you, the novelist, can do is bring your unique perspective to bear on that situation so that it strikes the reader with new and unexpected force. There's nothing new under the publishing sun. Except you.

Delicacy

Be careful when recycling deeply personal material garnered from interviews. There is no legal prohibition, unless you use the material in such a way that it is intended to defame (libel) someone, and since you are writing fiction anyway, that would be very hard to prove. But on ethical grounds – or even grounds of simple politeness – it will be best to 'clear' the use of such material with your source. Most people are surprisingly generous in opening up to novelists, knowing that they will not be identified in print either by name or direct quotation – but *because* they feel relaxed and expansive they may say more, and of a more personal nature, than they intended. So just check, either at the time of interview or of writing, that they are perfectly happy for something they've said to appear in your book.

I had a particularly salutary experience in this regard. When doing my research for *A Flower That's Free* I asked my parents to tell me everything they could remember about living on the island of Malta when it was under constant bombardment by the Italian and German air forces during the Second World War. They were a rich fund of firsthand, anecdotal material. Among many other stories, they described a night out at the officers' mess in Valetta with another young army couple. Their friends had a six-week-old baby whom they'd left in the charge of a teenage Maltese nanny. The girl had been given strict instructions that when the air-raid warning sounded, heralding the nightly pounding from the skies, she should take the baby into the slit trench in the back garden, batten down the covers and remain there until she heard the all-clear. She conscientiously obeyed the instructions. The air-raid began. A bomb hit the high wall that bordered the end of the garden, and tons of plaster and rubble fell on top of the slit trench. The girl and the baby perished. The house remained standing.

A story of tragic and terrible irony and one I used, almost word for word, in the novel. It all seemed such a long time ago, and any links with my family remote and very probably no longer in place.

Only a few years ago I accompanied my mother to a reunion of my father's old regiment at the Duke of York's Barracks in Chelsea. After the lunch I was approached by a distinguished-looking elderly man who told me that he'd read several of my books and enjoyed them. He remarked that he'd been particularly interested in the one which featured the siege of Malta, because he'd been there at the same time as my own parents, and he and his wife had been close friends of theirs.

I suddenly knew what was coming. It was like a bad dream – precognition did nothing to help me avert the impending disaster.

'You may be interested to know,' he said, his piercing blue eyes never leaving my face, 'that the baby was ours.'

I leave you to imagine how I felt.

As it happened, he could not have been kinder or more understanding, but that didn't stop me wanting the parquet to open up and swallow me, lock, stock and word processor.

How?

This falls into three categories: How do I find out what I want to find out? How do I retain it? How do I use it when I've got it?

How to find out

I've already indicated some of the avenues through which you can obtain background material, but the following list covers most of them:

- Books (histories, diaries, memoirs).
- Archives (museums, galleries, and personal and institutional collections).
- Interviews (people may have anecdotal material concerning the quite distant past, handed down by word of mouth).
- Cuttings.
- Radio and television (plays and documentaries – have tapes and videos to hand).
- Observation and listening – the mental box-room.
- Experiencing it yourself

Obviously the last one isn't available to you if you're writing about the distant past, but in the matter of other places and milieux it's one of the most effective ways of soaking up material.

A warning. Don't imagine that you can organise a free holiday in the Bahamas for yourself on the basis that you're going to set a novel there. It doesn't work like that. The idea and the story must come first. All those tired old jokes about 'When are you going to set a book in Reid's Hotel in Madeira, muggins?' usually come from people who imagine they may be able to get in on the act as research assistants/consultants.

However. . . if you are in a position to visit the place you're going to write about, then do so. Remember you'll have to pay up front – a novelist's expenses are tax-deductible, but not refundable by the publisher. If you've visited somewhere interesting in the past and it made a clear impression on you, then consider using it in the novel.

If for any reason you feel your plot demands a sequence set in Los Angeles, New York, Hong Kong or London – somewhere, in fact, which an international audience is going to know, or have read about extensively – try and fix it so that your character is seeing the place from a stranger's viewpoint, wide-eyed and naïve. That way you don't run the risk of trying to sound like a native and blowing it. Believe me, you can look up all the facts in the world, study bus routes, collect menus and programmes, listen to the dialogue in films, scan street maps and read guide-books – you can even have *been* there, for God's sake, for a limited time – and you can still get it wrong. Someone who really knows the place will

67

pick up the tell-tale hollow ring, their enjoyment will be constantly snagged by the not-quite-rightness of it all. This even applies to places in one's own country. Someone not familiar with London shouldn't try to bluff – too many people live there. And the Londoner shouldn't write about Newcastle as though it were her second home unless that's what it is. If you must write about Newcastle, then do so honestly – as it appears to a Londoner.

Visiting a place solely for the purposes of research is my favourite form of travelling. The sense of adventure, of purpose and discovery, gives a focus to the trip and an impetus to the journey which is quite simply not there in the average holiday. The satisfaction in seeing, smelling, hearing and tasting a place for yourself is immense, even more so if it's the site of some past event which till now you've only read about. For the novelist, nothing beats that 'This is where it actually happened' feeling. You look around you and see the lie of the land, the shape of the trees, the form of the buildings. It may be utterly different from how you imagined it, or how you knew it to be in those days – the thrill will still be as great.

How to retain it

A word on how best to retain these impressions. I don't believe that travel broadens the mind – rather the reverse. What seems to happen in nine cases out of ten is that new surroundings drive people into themselves. A change is certainly as good as a rest, but the benefits of the change may manifest themselves in thinking 'God, it's nice to be back!' when it's all over. The other manifestation is a desire to process the trip rather than to experience it – people with cameras and video-cameras glued to their faces, interminably scribbling notes, or hunched obsessively over their guide-books, may not actually be seeing anything.

Obviously you have to find your own way of recording experiences, but here's what I do. Keep asking yourself the question 'What is the purpose of this exercise?', to which the answer is, of course, 'To find out what it's like to be in this place'. That means finding out what it feels like, first and foremost. Facts and figures are easy to find out sitting at your desk. If you're **here**, **now**, then drink it all in.

Enjoy the experience as much as possible. Relax, but keep the writer's antennae waving. Soak it up. Eyes and ears wide open and mouth shut should be your maxim unless there's something specific you want to ask about. Eavesdrop shamelessly. Make a point of looking at the edges of things. If you're at some famous building or beauty spot, look at what's going on all around. Are there beggars? Tradespeople? Buskers? What are the other tourists like? How much litter is there? Traffic, if any? What does the attitude of the locals seem to be? Are there any jarring contradictions? Look for the details that only someone who was there in person would see. By all means take some pictures if you have a camera with you – even the most basic snaps are a useful *aide-mémoire* – but don't be a slave to the camera, and don't worry if you've left it in the hotel room. The pictures in your head are the most important ones. Don't make notes unless you absolutely have to – writing down something in a foreign language, for example. *Be* there.

The time to record is when you get back to base at the end of the day. Get out the pencil and paper and write like a maniac. Don't be selective. Write down every last thing you can remember from the moment you set out that morning. Don't worry about grammar, spelling or construction – this is just stream of consciousness stuff. You'll be astonished at the completeness of your recall if you do it that same evening. Sick it all up. All of it. This isn't for publication, or even for the scrutiny of anyone else. You yourself may never look at it again. It's chiefly a way of fixing images in your mind. And it works wonderfully. If you then – either at the time or when you get back to your desk – type out the scribbles, so much the better, you've hammered them home a bit more. You can paper-clip them together with any snaps, tickets, leaflets or whatever dating from the same time, and you've got a complete day 'preserved in aspic'.

The same goes for environments like places of work. If you're fortunate enough to be vouchsafed a privileged outsider's view of someone else's life, be alive to all the undercurrents, the body language, the atmosphere, the clothes, the decor – how the job is done is probably the least of it. An authentic representation of what it's like to be there will be far more convincing than a blow-by-blow account of the workings of the futures market, and more interesting to read.

How to use it

This is a question of understanding the correlation between your fictional narrative and the factual material underpinning it. Most often, where background is concerned, less is more – but it's got to be a well-chosen less, from a solid base of information and/or experience. If you want to dazzle, don't simply bang out all the facts and figures you can think of on your given subject. Don't reproduce the guide-book or the street map. Probably the last thing we notice about a new town is the names of the streets. We notice what's in the shops, and the smell, and the look of the buildings, and the way people are dressed, and how they sound. As pedestrians we notice the arrangements for crossing roads and what sort of drivers the natives are. Checking street names comes low down the list. Even if your character is a resident of the place, remember you're introducing the reader to this location for the first time. Do so in a rounded, complete way.

If you're writing about an area as it was at some point in the past, check the historical geography first – some buildings and streets were probably not even in existence then, others which are now defunct may have been flourishing thoroughfares. From the rest of your research, extract the stuff which is going to make your story live. Engage *all* the senses. And remember that the view of a place or event is coloured by the mood and personality of the person describing it. We'll cover this a bit more under 'Point of View', but for now just consider that the same London street will appear very different to a young girl going to meet her lover and, say, an elderly down-and-out with only months to live. You need enough information – and imagination – to view the scene through the appropriate 'lens'.

Story first

The same old cry – but if you can keep on reciting it, you'll be doing yourself a big favour.

In the case of research it sometimes works to get the first draft of your novel down on paper first, and then to fill in the background. This isn't such a shocking or perverse thing to do – a painter doesn't create a detailed background and then fill in the figures at the front, and there's no reason why you should. If you have the broad picture – the base of the pyramid – in your mind, you may well find it suits you better to storm ahead with the story and get it down on paper. Then you can research in more detail those areas which need it, and make adjustments to your second draft accordingly.

This method has the priceless advantage of keeping your priorities straight, and giving you less opportunity for pleasant procrastination in museums and libraries. It's all part of keeping the focus, which is what I want to talk about next.

7

THE TRIVIAL ROUND, THE COMMON TASK

'Don't get it right, get it written' is one of those creative-writing-class dictats which bears repeating. The best course of action for any writer is to write. Don't agonise over it – get on with it. Take it from me, you'll be remembered much more for what you say than how you say it.

But getting on with it can also be the hardest part of the whole creative process. There is nothing your average writer doesn't know about sorting paper clips, phoning the vet, watching the news, writing shopping lists, mending shelves, lunching in town, tidying cutlery drawers and changing sweaters – anything in fact, from the mindless to the blameless, to postpone the evil hour when work must be done.

Part of the problem, I suspect, is that writing a novel is such a long business, and feels so open-ended. It's hard to imagine, when you begin the first page, what it will be like to write the last one, or even whether you've got it in you to do it. Any novel is an emotional journey and as such it's hard to see it in terms simply of hours, weeks, pages and chapters.

Hard, but not impossible.

There's a whole range of devices you can employ to help you see it through. They are:

● Setting manageable targets.
● Finding a fixed place of work.
● Learning self-defence.
● Staying incommunicado
● Pressing the guilt button
● Giving yourself rewards.

- Breaking it down.
- Busting blocks.
- Pacing yourself.
- Letting off steam (while not running out of it).

Writing a blockbuster requires a sustained effort – intellectual, imaginative and physical. You'll have to be able to withstand a good deal of amiable ridicule and not let that, or fatigue, or self-doubt, or even boredom, get in the way of achieving your goal. Structures and strategies give you something to hang on to, and in the process may help you cling to sanity, too.

Setting manageable targets

One of the commonest reasons for novelists falling by the way-side is the feeling that it's all too much and they're simply never going to finish. In the case of the blockbuster this feeling is compounded by intermittent flushes of self-consciousness. As you sit before your keyboard, trying to conjure words from the ether in the vague hope that they will amount to something stupendous which will make your fortune and your reputation, you can't help but be aware of the rest of the world going about its business in the normal, useful, productive way: doing its sensible day job, paying into its pension scheme, saving for a rainy day, providing for its family, having a few beers with colleagues at lunchtime, and generally being part of the human race. At times like these it's easy to ask yourself: 'What am I doing? And why?' and to tell yourself: 'I don't have to do this.'

And of course you don't. You *chose* to. You elected to go for the big one, with all its attendant risks and responsibilities, and no-one can make you stick with it but you yourself. Be positive – you've embarked on something far more exciting and potentially rewarding than most other people you know. Are you going to let a bit of teasing and a few niggling doubts turn you aside from your objective?

You are? Okay, at least you're honest about it. Make a clean break, close this book right away and go and put on your grey suit . . .

73

If, as I hope and believe, you're not so easily deterred, then get to it, but don't terrify yourself into a state of quivering inertia before you've even started. Don't imagine you're going to have to burn the midnight oil, not to mention the candle at both ends, until further notice. Breaking your spirit on the wheel of overwork is a sure way of putting the skids under the whole enterprise. Rather, set aside a time – initially quite short, say half an hour – in which you're going to write. Make it the same time each day, or every other day, or even once a week – but *stick to it*. Consistency's the thing.

So do your half-hour without fail – and when the half-hour is up, stop.

That's right – no matter how well it's going, or how much more writing you think you've got inside you. Use an alarm clock if necessary. The idea is to make you begin your next session with a sense of pleasurable anticipation. Even if it's not going well, a short writing-time is less awesome and you're more likely to persist with it. Whatever the timetable, adhere to it rigidly. Set a time which suits you, when you're going to be reasonably fresh and stand some chance of getting peace and quiet, but then make sure you give the writing absolute priority at that time. Don't be seduced by things you'd rather do, nor shamed by things you think you should be doing. *This* is what you should be doing. Say no – to yourself and other people. It doesn't matter whether you've had a word published or not, you're writing and that makes you a writer. In less time than you might imagine, other people will fall in with this view. (On the other hand, if you insist you're a writer but do not write, they may quite justifiably be sceptical.)

So you're doing your half-hour a day. If at the end of a couple of weeks you're easily filling your allotted time and are beginning to find the self-imposed restrictions irksome, then ease them a little – perhaps up to an hour, but no more. Or, if you were writing only twice a week, make it four times a week. The trick is to keep yourself on a tight rein, eager and with energy to spare. If after a month things are still going well, up the time and/or frequency again, but always err on the side of caution. Because as well as keeping your enthusiasm alive, you're aiming to programme yourself to write at set times. If you begin to skip sessions through tiredness, boredom or sheer spinelessness, then you're on a slippery slope.

Finding a fixed place of work

The place is very nearly as important as the time in terms of programming. If a certain room, or chair, or table is associated with writing, then the mere act of taking up your position there will trigger something, even if it's only guilt (which anyway goes with the territory and is a wonderfully effective spur to work). The place doesn't have to be a tranquil, book-lined room with a breathtaking view, solely dedicated to the production of deathless prose. It can be a kitchen, bedroom, dining room, garden shed or garage, provided that at the time you elect to write it's going to be empty, and not susceptible to invasion by other people. In my experience quite a high level of noise is tolerable provided it's going on on the other side of a door and isn't accompanied by any actual interruptions. The door is a psychological as well as a physical barrier. Others in the house need to know that the closed door means No Admittance.

Perhaps because I used to work in a busy editorial office I've always, until recently, been able to work against a certain amount of activity and hubbub. Provided there weren't any seriously acrimonious confrontations taking place, or any noisy, unchecked weeping, I could write. In the past year, however, my concentration has become a more delicate plant and I betake myself each morning to a rented attic in the neighbouring village. This attic is over the garage of friends. It's cold, undecorated, uncurtained, and has no heating or running water. *However*, it also contains no telephone, fax, domestic animals or dependent relatives. I've installed a convector heater, I take a thermos, and I write. Answering the call of nature involves a hike through another two attics, down vertiginous unlighted stairs, through a spider-webbed barn, round the corner of the barn, across a large yard, into the main house and down a long corridor to the loo, so I'm tempted to put off even that for as long as possible. There are no distractions, so even on bad days I can bore myself into getting on with the novel. Be-

75

cause in order to leave I have to walk through someone else's work-attic, I'm shamed into putting in a respectable number of hours. Because I do nothing else in the attic but write the current novel, I'm conditioned to it. When I sit down at my trestle table beneath the unshaded light bulb that stirs slightly in the draught I know I'll be prompted into writing sooner or later, rather as one is prompted, sooner or later, into fastening one's seat belt in the car.

Learning self-defence

When you've established a pattern, and reckon you've programmed yourself to work in a certain place at set times, you'll confront what is potentially a far harder task – to convince other people that you are serious.

There is a wilful individualism in the urge to write. It involves a deliberate and determined shutting-away of oneself, and a self-belief which may seem like arrogance. All this can be threatening to someone who does not understand it, and that someone is often the person with whom you share your life.

Partners and spouses generally break down into two types – the supportive and the uncomprehending. The first type is to be treasured, the second can't help but be an unsettling influence, with behaviour ranging from the petulant to the downright undermining. If you are unlucky enough to be saddled with the second sort then sooner or later it's likely you'll be faced with a High Noon of the creative spirit – a straight choice between your writing and your partner. I wouldn't dream of interfering. But bear in mind that if writing's really important to you, then giving it up is likely to make you bitter and twisted, and horribly resentful towards whoever is the cause of your giving up. So you might wind up losing both.

I'm about to make a sexist remark, so if you think it's going to give you an attack of the vapours, or raise your blood pressure to dangerous levels, turn over a couple of pages now. There is strong anecdotal evidence to support the theory that men seem to have more problem with their partners writing than women do. I just thought I'd mention it . . .

Friends and acquaintances will respond to training. Firm and insistent is the name of the game here. If you don't take yourself seriously, no-one else will. Callers, both on the phone and in person, must be discouraged. Tell them politely but unequivocally that you are writing, and suggest another time when you will be able to speak to them. Ideally this information should be disseminated beforehand – prevention is better than cure. Then if they don't act on it, either through forgetfulness or because they're being deliberately obtuse, you can be a touch more forceful. Genuine emergencies apart, don't make any exceptions to the rule – you'll be making a rod for your own back.

Staying incommunicado

If you work somewhere where there is a telephone – well, it's better not to. I know there's nothing that thickens the arteries quicker than listening to a phone ringing, unanswered. And an answering machine doesn't necessarily help. If it's someone you want to speak to, the sound of their voice is as alluring as any siren-song, especially if the book's not going well. Unfortunately the sound of the telephone has come to assume a huge urgency and importance to most writers. After all, it just *might* be your agent or publisher with news of a film offer . . . or translation rights . . . or a five-figure American deal . . . or a serialisation on prime-time television.Solitary little souls that we are, we believe that every sound from the outside world is potentially thrilling news. Experience will also have shown that this is rarely the case. If it is your agent or publisher calling it will be to tell you of the wizard price they're in a position to offer you on your remaindered titles, or to explain that they omitted to deduct commission and VAT from your last payment and will have to do so twice on the current one. Quite honestly, it's best to be somewhere where you can't even hear a telephone. If this is impossible, then have one right next to you and answer it immediately – but resist the urge to talk for longer than about two minutes. At least that way you won't waste additional time angsting, dithering, deliberating and finally rushing to the phone only for it to stop ringing the moment you get there so that you then have to ring all the likely suspects to find out who it was.

The same goes for faxes. In fact the buzz of a fax can be even more seductive than the phone. The moment it rings you'll find yourself watching for the heading to appear. Even if it's for someone else you'll probably wind up reading it, human nature being what it is. You can't stop a fax invading your life – it belches forth its messages whether you want them or not. The fax is an absolute definition of invasion of privacy. So if the magic machine can be elsewhere, so much the better. If you must work in the same room with it, check messages at once, and if they're not for you, look the other way.

Pressing the guilt button

If a large part of your day is spent doing a 'proper job' then you needn't read the next bit. If, however, you are unemployed, or a wife and mother, or have courageously given up the day job in order to write, pay close attention. You may have trained the neighbours to accept that you're a writer, and that you work set hours. But they will always be lying in wait to catch you out. Sightings of you in the supermarket, at the pub, walking the dog or at your daughter's netball match will be the occasion of a good deal of jeering along the lines of: 'Call that a proper job?/We should be so lucky/Doing a spot of research at the local?' Now, it doesn't matter two hoots what people think, and you will soon, if you haven't already done so, develop the hide of a pachyderm to withstand these jibes. But let me offer you a mechanism to help you resolve any uneasiness you feel.

For a start, writing is not a job exactly like any other, and we sell ourselves short if we say it is. No matter how conscientious you are about your writing, there are going to be times when you have to leave it for a bit. Going for a walk, shopping, seeing a friend, any of them may be the displacement activity which help the knot of difficulty relax and loosen. You'll soon learn to feel the difference between a quite justifiable break from the desk, and skiving. If you are skiving, be big enough to admit it to yourself and anyone else. If you're not, don't be fazed by any remarks.

The blockbuster is going to be a part of your life for as long as it's going on, whether or not you're sitting at the desk. The characters, their story and background are going to be in your head and heart for a long time. You'll find they're never far from the surface of your thoughts. The imaginative juices work on them all the time. The process is continuous. Try to think of the novel as a large shady tree, or giant umbrella, which will cast its shade over your life for the duration of the writing. Just because you get on with the other things in your life, it doesn't mean that the novel isn't there or is being ignored. When I was writing *The Flowers of the Field* I was in a more or less permanent state of contained excitement, whether or not I was actually writing. I mentally hugged myself. I lost weight. It was like being in love. So don't let anyone else press the guilt button. That's your prerogative, and only you will know when it's appropriate.

Giving yourself rewards

Have them. Everyone works better with a little encouragement and a few incentives, and as a writer, there's no-one to provide them but you.

Of course I'm not talking anything extravagant here. But if you set yourself a target and achieve it, then allow yourself a glass of wine, an hour in the sunshine, or the opportunity to hoover the inside of the car – whatever lights your candle. Positive reinforcement can only be helpful.

Don't, however, imagine that mentally punishing yourself for not achieving the target is going to have the same effect. A sense of failure accompanied by self-recrimination is a recipe for inertia. Try to see the glass as half-full rather than half-empty. So the writing hasn't gone so well – never mind, you must have achieved *something* today, and a bad day's writing doesn't make you a bad person. You'd have bad days wherever you were working, but the difference is that in an office, bad days are swallowed up in the routine. You're in salaried employment whether you're clinching the deal of the century or picking your feet. Writing doesn't have that security. So just take responsibility for the bad day and make sure the next one's better. Don't wallow.

Breaking it down

You'll have gathered by now that the thrust of this chapter is to-wards keeping going. If there's anything that can be done to make the day-to-day business of writing easier, then you should do it.

I've never thought it practical to say 'I'll write so many pages a day', for the simple reason that some pages are much more labour-intensive than others. There will be occasions when to have written one is a significant achievement and others when a dozen practically write themselves. For this reason it's often more productive to set different kinds of objective.

The outline you wrote for yourself will remind you of the purpose of each chapter – where it takes the action and the characters, and to what effect. Before you begin a new chapter, write another short outline breaking the chapter down into its component scenes. By a scene I mean a section of the story that's complete in itself and is separated from what precedes and follows it by a double space. Make sure each scene is as tight and gripping as you can make it, and that it has a precise function in the narrative. Keep in mind where the chapter's taking the reader in terms of narrative tension. The scenes will vary considerably in length – chapters in a blockbuster are generally long but well broken-up – from half a page to several pages.

Set yourself targets in terms of these scenes rather than in rigid numbers of pages. Tell yourself you'll get a short one done before lunch – or alternatively that you'll complete a long one in two days. This not only gives you something to work towards, but it's more organic. It's got more to do with the narrative curve and the way you think than with simply covering paper. The ten-pages-a-day school of writing is mechanistic. Much more important and more exciting, in my view, is the covering of the story as you see it in your head. That way you'll have made real progress in the narrative journey – the creative process.

Busting blocks

For once it's not success but survival I'm talking about here. The kind of blocks I have in mind are those which most authors confront at some time or other. They come in all shapes and sizes, from the terrifying inability to start the book at all, to the feeling that one doesn't know 'what to to put' because one has quite simply run out of words.

The second kind is the commoner. It's unpleasant because it can ambush us at any time, sometimes between one page and the next, and can have a horribly undermining effect. You may be experiencing a little difficulty in tackling a particular scene – then suddenly it's the following day and you still haven't cracked it. A terrible anxiety creeps over you – are you up to the job? What are you playing at? Should you be writing at all, let alone attempting to write a blockbuster?

This feeling must be summarily dispelled. Think of the block as a hobgoblin to which you give credence by acknowledging it. All you're experiencing is a little local difficulty. If two days have gone by and the work isn't yielding to pressure (or to the stark terror you're probably feeling), then take a break for a day. Give yourself a complete change: go to France for the day, buy a hat, paint the window frames, ask for a rise, fire your secretary, clean out the pond. Free your mind of the novel and its accompanying problems.

The next day, sit back down at the desk at the appointed time and start to write. Given the horrors that are attacking you, that may sound like being told to walk on water. Well, yes, an act of faith is exactly what it is. Don't stop to think – let the subconscious take over. Write *something* about the characters and their circumstances, listen to their voices and let your story lead you.

Writing, particularly a sustained effort of writing, is a state of mind. You know it's true, because you're now in the habit of thinking of yourself as a writer. So sit down and be one. One nifty little trick is to pretend you're in a film. (This is embarrassing to confess, but it does work.) See yourself as the camera might see you. Say it's the end of a Hitchcock-esque thriller in which a writer has been in truly appalling danger, stalked by a crazed killer, men-

81

aced by unseen forces of hatred and evil, the action culminating in a heartstopping chase through deserted night-time streets. Now the danger has passed. Life goes on. Dawn breaks. The writer and her work are reunited. Peaceful, productive, protected – and inspired – the writer sits at her desk and picks up the threads. The camera watches her through the window, closes in on the intent face and rapt expression, the hands moving at first tentatively, then with increasing urgency, across the keyboard. The camera observes for a few seconds more, then draws back from the desk, and from the house, and pans away across rooftops and fields to swelling music as the credits roll.

Being 'a writer'

When I said write anything, of course I lied. Not quite anything will do. Write something enjoyable. Let rip. Don't worry about order and control, that's for little people. Just now it's vital you see yourself as the creator of a blockbuster, firing on all cylinders and letting the imagination roll.

For this it may be necessary to abandon, for the moment, the scene you were originally writing, the one that was giving you so much bother, and to write one that is begging to be written. It may be large and operatic or subtle and poignant. What defines it here is that you are going to enjoy it.

Be the star in your own film. Act 'being a writer'. Like that corny old advice about forcing yourself to smile – if you can manage it, it can actually make you feel that there's something to smile about.

A worse sort of block is the one that prevents you getting started at all. The solution here also has to do with not getting stuck in one's thinking. Stop imagining yourself beating your puny fists on some huge, unyielding edifice, or feeling its cold surface for cracks and a way through. Back off and walk round it. (I'm big on visualisation.) The block is probably not very thick, and will appear different – or even vanish altogether – depending on how you look at it. Don't get into one particular mind-set about your novel. It doesn't *have* to be one particular way. Who's in charge?

Remember, what you're trying to do is free yourself, rediscover spontaneity – inspiration if you like – and by feeling and thinking like a victim you're creating the opposite effect.

An example

I became horribly stuck following publication of *The Flowers of the Field*. In theory I was in an ideal situation – my first novel was a bestseller, I had a publisher positively panting for the next one, money up front – but could I get started? Could I hell. The very factors which made my situation enviable also made it paralysing.

For one thing, I'd lost the energising surprise factor which made the first novel so thrilling to write. I was no longer the new kid on the block, but a professional writer with a contract, and an eager publisher anticipating a profitable sequel. I'd talked about it – we'd talked about it – everyone had talked about it – ideas had been batted about like ping-pong balls – everything was out there in the public domain being exposed to the harsh light of day. I felt beached.

The success of the first book was like a literary Old Man of the Sea clinging to my back, getting heavier and heavier. How could I possibly follow that? I didn't know how I'd done it in the first place, so how the dickens was I going to reproduce it?

I won't bore you with a chronicle of the nigh-on two and a half years during which I languished in the wilderness, unable to get going and so lacking in confidence that I seriously thought I wouldn't write again. The point is that when I did finally crack it and make a start, it was because I'd found a different way of approaching the novel. It didn't have to be *Flowers II* – it could and should be a separate and distinct exercise. I had the advantage of being able to use some characters which were familiar, both to me and at least some of my readers, but what would make this novel jump was not what was the same, but what was different about it. I needed an exciting new character through whose eyes to view the story. I thought of people – especially women – that I knew, and took the characteristics of one of them as the model for Kate Kingsley. Her spiky, sometimes perverse independence and her fierce but largely untried emotions were exactly what was needed to breathe new life into what was beginning to feel like a dead horse. The whole novel started to look and feel different. I was away.

Just remember that in trying to overcome blocks and difficulties, what you're attempting is to recreate freshness and excitement – to remind yourself of why you're a writer, and why you embarked on this novel in particular. In truth (as I'm sure you realised) I'm against cold-blooded mechanistic approaches and methods. When you're stuck, what you need is a fillip, not a monkey-wrench.

One more thing

For heaven's sake don't worry about what other people are up to. The obsessive analysing of other writers' routines and methods can damage your health, and that of your book. For every published writer who sits down daily at 6 a.m. to write continously till 2 p.m. (when she breaks for macrobiotic salad and spring water), and who would think it shame to rise from the desk having written anything less than 3,000 words, there'll be another two who think themselves lucky if they manage a couple of decent paragraphs before knocking off at noon. The difference is that the second lot keep quiet about it. Through a process of trial and error you'll find the *modus operandi* that suits you. If you're making progress and enjoying it – most of the time – that's plenty. Have faith in your own working methods. There are plenty of people out there with the same dreams and ambitions as you, and they're not doing a darn thing about it.

8

JACKANORY

'I'll tell you a story of Jackanory,
And now my story's begun;
I'll tell you another of Jack and his brother,
And now my story's done.'

That's how the rhyme goes. The scenario's a touch short on tension and conflict, but it does at least express one plain fact: story
is everything. A fellow-panellist on a Radio Four talk-show turned
to me one week when I'd done particularly badly and said: 'Hard
luck. You know, it's so much easier to say something if you've got
something to say.' Ouch.

Writing is not an end in itself. The comment: 'It's really well
written, but I couldn't get into it,' probably means it's *not* all that
well written. You write in order to communicate something. If in
doing so you are fluent, economical and vivid, that's great. But flu-
ency and brilliance are not the *purpose* of the writing. The story is.

Your aim is to hold your audience spellbound as you relate your
tale. But of course you're not actually 'telling' this story. You're
at one remove. You have no glittering eye, no thrilling voice, no
gestures or facial expressions, to help you – just the written word.
So it follows that you must engage the reader's imagination as
fully as possible with the resources at your disposal. You cannot
afford to be dull.

Narrative pull and tension

When we talked about planning I explained the difference between
story and plot. In this chapter I make no apology for merging the

two once more. After all, the process of learning, and of explanation, is often one of deconstructing, demonstrating, and then reconstructing again.

You've taken a series of events and a collection of characters, framed a proposition or hypothesis, selected a background, and then plotted a course to create what is now, we hope, an utterly compelling story. 'Story' was strictly chronological and sequential – one thing following on another in a straight line. 'Plot' – we'll call it story from now on – has texture, light and shade, complexity, richness. But more than any of these it should have narrative tension.

'Tension' in this context does not mean a well-coiffed blonde hanging by her magenta nails from the edge of a cliff, or an innocent moppet playing with a bag full of dynamite. Of course it can be those. But it is first and foremost something far more important: the page-turning quality of your narrative – the 'pull'. I prefer 'pull' to 'drive', because a sure sign of the story going well is that you, the author, feel pulled along by it, drawn to write the next scene, and the next – as the reader, we hope, will be drawn to read it. If you feel that in some way you are 'behind' the story, forcing or 'pushing' it along, then something's not working. You're trying to impose solutions from outside rather than grow them organically from within. It may simply be that you need a rest, but more likely there is some inherent fault in the way the story or characters are constructed. This is why full, early consideration of character and motivation pays dividends.

At least some of the narrative tension can be set up at the planning stage. In fact, this is why I'm an inveterate planner. If I know where I'm going, what surprises and *coups de théâtre* are in store along the way, and what the wonderful and satisfying ending is to be, I can orchestrate my effects as I choose: diminuendo here, crescendo there, and introduce themes and variations. Narrative tension provides freedom for manoeuvre without the risk of aimless meandering, and this in turn communicates itself to the reader, who knows she is in safe hands.

The bad news is that narrative tension is a lot harder to achieve in a massive, sweeping, crowded novel of 450-plus pages than in a taut urban thriller of 200, but it is doubly important. If you lose your thread in an enterprise of this scale, then the reader will un-doubtedly lose hers. Here are a few simple dos and don'ts, an *aide mémoire* to help keep you on course:

- Don't over-use flashback, or back-tracking. It has its place; keep it there. Keep the story moving forward.
- Ask yourself at regular intervals: Whose story is this? What do they want? How close are they to getting it?
- Remind yourself of your theme – bear it in mind, like a tune you've got on the brain.
- Don't allow important scenes to slip by – give them full value. Show them to the reader as they happen (more of this shortly).
- When describing people, places or settings, ask yourself: How much of this actually adds to the reader's necessary knowl-edge (knowledge that will enhance their appreciation of plot and character)? Then prune.
- Bear in mind that the author of a would-be blockbuster wishes to reach as many people as possible, and that you are there-fore more than most the servant of the reader. Always ask yourself: What is the most gripping/entertaining/harrowing/dramatic way of doing this? Then do it.
- The summation of all the above: STORY FIRST.

Voice

The storytelling voice is what marks out the million-seller from the also-ran. You may never be reviewed in the 'qualities', you may never be heard on posh arts programmes, nor have your views on 'Whither the modern novel?' elicited by people with plummy voices . . . But if you can write an opening line like 'Last night I dreamed I went to Manderley again . . . ', and then press your advantage with a terrific story, the readers will find you, and they will tell other readers, and you will sell. The fact is that competent writing, provided it doesn't actually jar, will go largely unremarked if what it says is sufficiently remarkable. If the writing is excel-lent as well, that's a bonus.

The art of the storyteller is essentially intimate. Publishers love the row of noughts, the extravagant claims and the talk of thousands . . . millions . . . as though the author were standing on top of Nelson's Column and bawling at the top of her lungs. You and I know that the opposite is true. No-one wants to be shouted at. Even – in fact especially – a blockbuster, no matter how mighty its theme or how panoramic its canvas, must give the impression that you are sitting in a secluded place and inviting the reader to sit near you.

'Come over here,' you say, 'and sit by me. Relax. I am going to tell you a story, and no one can tell it quite the way I can.'

It may be true that there are only a finite number of basic storylines. How many is neither here nor there. What marks out the blockbuster novel is the strength and individuality of the author's storytelling voice.

Most authors will tell you that 'finding their voice' was an important breakthrough. It marks the writing's transition from the conscious to what the psychologists call the procedural – it becomes not a device, but the most natural, fluid way to tell your story. Once you've found your voice it won't desert you. You may in the fullness of time write different types of novel, and use the voice in different ways, but it will remain distinctly and discernibly yours.

An example

When I found myself with a contract to write *The Flowers of the Field,* I was mad keen to start the book, but also terrified of doing so. It was hard to see how I, a hard-pressed mother of two under-fives, was going to be able to produce the huge and impressive novel of my imagination.

I didn't do all that much research initially, but one of the books I dipped into was one of those wonderful Edwardian 'with-mule-and-notebook-through-the-Sudan' kind of travel chronicles. The author photograph on the flyleaf showed a straight-backed, big-busted lady with a forbidding expression. One suspected that no matter how hot the Sudan, she never removed either the expression or her thornproof tweeds.

I didn't read the whole book – it had virtually nothing to do with the content of my novel – but something about the way it was written opened up possibilities. The author was strong, determined, doughty, entirely admirable in fact – but the reverse telescope of time made her even more interesting. I saw that it would be possible to write an historical novel that was completely true to itself and observed all the dramatic unities, but that also invited the modern reader to marvel at how certain things had come about. I didn't want to say simply 'here's what happened' – I wanted to have an angle.

In the way that the best teachers are not totally unbiased or objective, but colour their subject with their individuality, so the best storytellers have an angle. That doesn't mean they peddle a particular political line, but they have a way of looking at the world which may correspond to or differ sharply from our own, but which speaks to us.

Point of view

The storyteller has two alternatives – the first-person narrative, which has the advantage of immediacy and directness; or the third-person, which enables you to be the omniscient author, moving from place to place, and from character to character, at will.

I was about to say that the second method is more suited to the blockbuster – and immediately remembered *Jane Eyre* and *Rebecca*, both told, triumphantly, in the first person.

However, I think they may be the exceptions which prove the rule. The term 'blockbuster', with everything we understand by it, is a modern one, implying certain conventions and given factors, most of which we've explored in earlier chapters. You might very well write a novel in the first person which subsequently became a blockbuster, and I'd be the last to discourage you from giving it a go. But if we're looking at the laws of probability, we must conclude that the third-person narrative is generally more suited to the telling of a long story, with many characters, set over a considerable period and against a variety of backgrounds.

The third person gives you freedom, flexibility and power. The story is quite literally in your hands. You can from time to time set aside certain characters and parts of the action, and highlight others. There are more options open to you than there are to the first-person narrator. But perversely the very things which make this kind of narrative desirable also create pitfalls. For whereas the first-person narrator has one, and only one, clear and distinct point of view, the third-person narrator has many. And her choice of which to assume, and when, is vital to the effectiveness of the story.

You know by now whose story you are telling. That person is not only the most important person in the novel, but also the reader's touchstone, the means by which she gets the feel of how things are going, and the emotional temperature. It follows that this character is the one who will be 'onstage' most, and whose point of view you are most likely to adopt. It is her attitude, thinking and frame of mind, filtered of course by your narrative voice – your opinion of her – which will colour most of the story. The readers must never be in any doubt as to whose side you, and therefore they, are on. It's not absolutely essential that this character be sympathetic but, especially in a blockbuster, it's likely, because right will almost certainly prevail in some sense.

However, in the course of a long book you will have many scene changes, and many scenes which do not include your central character. In fact as I've already indicated, it's a good idea to let the central character 'rest' from time to time. A different point of view gives you another angle and will subtly alter the way you write – your style. This variety is not only of intrinsic benefit to the book, it will also help you in the writing process, and be pleasing to the reader. These days no writer can afford to ignore the influence of films and television, where scenes change, angles alter and perspectives shift all the time and in no more than a split second, while never leaving us in the slightest doubt as to who is at the centre of the story.

The following extract from *An Imperfect Lady* shows Adeline and her last and greatest love, Charlie Farrell, approaching a crisis in their relationship. We see first her perspective, then his. There's a poignant irony in the discrepancy between the two:

She was aching in every joint as she climbed the steps to the front door and let herself in. She could hear the phone ringing as she did so, a hard, peremptory intrusive sound, but by the time she was inside Charlie had answered it. She closed the door quietly, but he knew she was there and held out his arm to her as he listened to whoever it was. Wearily she went to him and laid her face on his shoulder, feeling his hand warm and confiding on the back of her neck, beneath her hair. Tears of sheer debility welled and oozed from her eyes and feeling them he stroked her.

'No,' he said sharply, in a voice unlike his own. 'No, sorry. Nothing at all. Thank you.'

He said 'thank you' in a brutally rude and dismissive tone. Then he depressed the cradle once, and laid the receiver, buzzing angrily like a fly on its back, on the table. Adeline had had enough of being rude and dismissive herself. To hear Charlie doing it for her was like receiving the most romantic of gifts.

'Thanks . . .' she whispered. 'Thanks. God, how I hate them.'

'They're only doing their job.'

'Don't defend them!'

'It's you I'm trying to defend.'

'I know and I'm sorry. I'm sorry you had to find out in this way what I should have told you long ago.'

'Sssh . . .'

His arm round her waist, he led her up the stairs and into the bedroom. It was in darkness and he didn't turn on a lamp.

'Come on,' he said, 'take your things off and get into bed.'

She pulled away from him, rubbing her eyes and forehead, summoning her resolve.

'I don't want to sleep just yet, I want to talk!'

'Sleep for a while, then. You'll talk better if you do. Phone's off the hook and I'm here to look after you.'

He slipped her jacket off her shoulders and then knelt to coax her feet out of her shoes. There was something in the sight of him kneeling there, doing her this small tender service, which unmanned her completely and she gave herself up to his ministrations, his undoing of buttons and zips, his slipping her nightdress over her head. She thought she'd never loved him more, and it was when she needed to love him most. The rightness of it was a comfort to her. As she slid down between the sheets she asked: 'What will you do?'

'I'm not tired. I had some kip earlier. Don't worry. I'll be here whenever you wake up.'

In fact, she slept until six, when brilliant early morning sun fell full on her face to wake her, and though Charlie wasn't beside her she could hear him downstairs, clinking cups, making tea. She felt lapped and protected by his care. Rested now, in the early, sunlit morning, she'd tell him what she had to do and they'd begin again.

Charlie watched his own hands as they put the tea things on the tray. They were perfectly steady, the movements precise and delicate. He felt slightly distanced from himself. It was like being drunk, except that he was clear-headed. He was so absorbed in his own problem that he felt no conflict between his sympathy for Adeline and his urgent need to capitalize on her predicament. His only niggling concern was that the eliciting of this last kindness from her might postpone his departure. So fine was the balance between loving and leaving Adeline that he could scarcely distinguish between the two. He carried the tray up the stairs, and nudged open the bedroom door with his foot. Adeline was sitting up against the pillows, the back of her right wrist against her forehead, as if shading her eyes: she was smiling. She looked beautiful, and tired. Her beauty tugged at Charlie's heart, but seemed also to vindicate him. After all, he was a swine. She deserved better. He'd be doing her a favour by going.

You can change point of view as often as you like, provided you 'return' to your central character and touch base with her in between. Remember she's the lodestone; without her prevailing and pervasive point of view the others will bob about unanchored, and be less effective.

However, be very wary of changing point of view within a scene. Not only is it difficult to do successfully, it's confusing to the reader. I have already described a 'scene' as a self-sufficient section of the narrative flanked by double spaces. You can insert a 'flash' of someone else's point of view in a given scene provided you similarly contain and separate it by double spaces. Obviously there's only a limited number of times you can do this without breaking the flow, so it needs handling with extreme caution and restraint. On the whole, if your central character is present, then use her point of view. If you wish to show her as she is perceived by someone else, then arrange it so that she is being observed – through a window, in a busy street, or across a crowded room.

Conflict

The drama in any situation, real or fictional, derives from the re-
sounding clash of interests. Conflicting personalities, motivations,
ideologies, ambitions, loyalties – even the conflicting emotions
harboured by one individual –are what make up the complex weave
of a good story.

If, for instance, your heroine is driven by the need to do good
among the Yardies of Jamaica, what happens if she falls passionately in love with a) a leading gangster or b) a hard-nosed police
chief (Beloved Enemy again) – or, oh yes, c) a celibate Roman
Catholic missionary? What happens? Great stuff is what. Drama,
both actual and internal. Which way will our girl go, ultimately?
For selfless spiritual fulfilment in a dangerous sewer of criminality
and vice? Or for the equally risky uncharted waters of emotional
entanglement?

It figures that if characters get whatever they want from life in
the first twenty pages there's not a lot left to say, except "so what?"
If Romeo and Juliet get it together and effect a reconciliation between their warring familes in Scene One, then that's about it.
Nice but dull. Not to mention short. So set up conflict. Seeds you
sow early in the narrative can be left to germinate, and flower
much later – that's plot, the arrangement of events for maximum
impact, remember? Did your hero suffer a traumatic incident as a
child which is going to come back to haunt him later in life? Does
your heroine have a hidden phobia or weakness which someone
else will be able to exploit? Who are his natural enemies? Who is
her unexpected rival? What about family relationships (always
vexed)? And friends who may turn up on the 'wrong' side at some
later stage in the story? What about outside forces – war, famine,
revolution, natural disaster? Any or all of these can create the conflict without which there is no drama.

Plain sailing is awfully like being becalmed.

Show and Tell

Here are two ways of writing the same short scene, in which the contents of a certain letter are pivotal to the plot:

Version 1
When John came in he ignored Lucy's greeting and went straight to the desk. He took out the letter which had arrived that morning. When he'd studied it he tucked it behind the silk handkerchief in his breast pocket, and then sat down opposite her. His wife asked him about his day but he was non-committal. They sat in silence. He didn't know how to tell her what must be told. She was more worried than she could say.

Version 2
Lucy looked up as her husband came into the room. 'Hallo, darling.'

He didn't reply, but went over to the desk and took out the letter which had arrived that morning. The silence grew oppressive as he studied it and then slotted it into his breast pocket behind the silk handkerchief, the one she'd given him for Christmas.

'How was the day?' she asked. 'Fraught?'

'Not unduly.'

His face was drawn and grey. Lucy knew she'd have to wait for whatever he wanted to say. She twiddled her wedding ring. Her stomach churned with anxiety.

I've overplayed my hand rather here, because the second version is, I believe, more interesting on several counts. (By the way, it looks longer only because I've inserted dialogue – the actual difference in length between the two versions is only fifteen words.)

The main thing to notice about the second version is that it *shows* John and Lucy in action. We are in the room with them, at the precise moment that the action takes place, and we're watching it as it unfolds. In version one, the time travelled is unclear, and the action is merely reported – we are *told* about it. The result is flatter, toneless – duller. Wherever you can, show the events as they happen, or show their effect on the characters, or show the characters changing and interacting. Your object should be to enable the reader to see for herself, rather than merely to tell her something is so. Apart from being more absorbing and dramatic, it's also more effective storytelling; what we observe for ourselves we understand and retain, it hooks into both our imagination and our memory.

I should add as an aside here that the second version is more compelling by virtue of using direct speech, and also because it has a clear point of view – Lucy's. We see events through her eyes and feel her anxiety, which adds tension to the action.

Changing gear

So we've established that for all key scenes Show is preferable to Tell. But key scenes are arias. An opera entirely composed of arias would be enough to give anyone aural indigestion. So with novels. What about the 'recitative'? The information that needs to be put across with the minimum of fuss? The best way to do that is to tell.

Finding the shift between these two storytelling gears is a trick the blockbuster-writer does well to learn. It figures that if you're telling a story on a grand scale you need to be able to alter the focus from the general to the particular swiftly and seamlessly as the plot dictates. There's nothing wrong with putting the reader in the picture about what's going on in the world – giving them a global view of Wall Street/the state of the war/the advertising industry/the world of plastic surgeons/fourteenth-century peasants/the court of James I/the breeding of Arab horses. In fact, a certain amount of basic information is essential, especially if the world into which you're inviting the reader is distant in time, geography or experience. You need to be able to set out certain salient facts – and by implication your own or your characters' position on them – in a succinct, effective way, before beginning, or resuming, the story. The following is the scene from *The Flowers of the Field* in which Thea finds, on the outbreak of war, that her younger sister has eloped with the tutor of the family with whom they're staying:

The storm rumbled and flashed round the Wolzsee; the water grew choppy and the trees stirred and sighed in the gathering wind. Having done what packing she could, Thea made her way to Dulcie's room. She wondered how much her sister had taken with her. No elopement could possibly run its course under the burden of the luggage that Dulcie normally carried.

95

The room was neat. The small things had been taken from the dressing table—brushes, combs, bottles of scent—but the wardrobe revealed ,most of Dulcie's clothes still hanging there, like ghosts. Thea gathered them up and laid them on the bed. She had better pack them. No one else would.

The empire through which Peter de Laszlo shepherded her an irritable and apprehensive young English lady was one in the grip of war fever. The assassination of the Archduke Franz Ferdinand and the Countess Sophie was simply the final straw that broke the back of the monarchy's patience. The crime of Gavrilo Princip and his handful of grammar-school braves was just a symptom, an eruption on the already disfigured skin of Austria-Hungary's political life.

The assassination at Sarajevo, it was universally agreed must be seen as a challenge not only to the Empire's position as ruler of Bosnia but to her declining prestige as a great power. Touchily, Austria-Hungary's statesmen demanded overt and immediate vindication. Her huge army, accumulated during peacetime in order to preserve peace, unbalanced her so that the slightest movement could cause a military landslide.

Dulcie did not believe in war. But, though she could ignore the war-clouds, she could not prevent them gathering, and as she and Peter made their way west to Paris her nerves were torn to shreds by their continued threatening presence. She became plaintive and belligerent by turns. Peter noticed that the spirited cavalier air she affected with such style in the drawing-room and on the dance floor deserted her with alarming rapidity when she was obliged to spend an hour or two on a train. And her looks, dependent as they were on her humour, fluctuated proportionately.

However, the die had been cast, and on 2 July they reached Paris and found a couple of rented rooms in the Place d'Agnette in Montmartre. The bohemian flavour of their new address resuscitated Dulcie's flagging spirits like a whiff of salts. She at once began to recover. Here she was further away from all the tedious war-talk, and Paris had long held sway in her imagination as the capital of taste and fashion. She still had some of her holiday allowance, and Peter had his private income; they could live like kings. Borne on a wave of optimism she went out and purchased two smart dresses and then sat down in high good humour to write to her relations, exhorting them not to worry about her. It did not for one second occur to her that the inconvenience to themselves might be greater than any imagined harm to her person, or that they might have greater or more pressing worries than for her safety. She was a creature of the moment. She had run away to Paris, for what she supposed was love. The horrors of the journey behind her, she allowed herself to bask in the fulfilment of this long-cherished dream.

' . . .*As merry as a robin, that sings on a tree,*' she hummed to herself as she lay in bed at eleven o'clock in the morning, a week after their arrival. They had not been in the rooms long enough for much dirt to have accumulated, they ate out or not at all, they had paid the concierge a month's rent in advance. Geraniums flowered on the little iron balcony and the smell of strong coffee floated through from the other room; the perfect love-nest.

Peter put his head round the door. 'I'm going out.'

From this you'll see that I prefer not to begin with the general, but with the particular. Most authors experience the urge to set out loads of background material early on in order to get it 'out of the way', forgetting that in doing so they run the risk of boring the reader rigid, and possibly disaffecting her altogether. By the time they get to specifics – character and action – in Chapter Two, there may be no one there to hear . . . In many cases when you look back at the opening of your blockbuster you will find it profitable to swap round Chapters One and Two. After all, if you begin with the real business of the story, direct, close-up and enthralling, your reader will be sufficiently hooked to accept, and more easily digest, the information you give her later.

If you want to begin with generalities, be bold. Scene-setting doesn't have to be dry and turgid. One of the most stirring openings to a novel is that of *A Tale of Two Cities* – 'It was the best of times, it was the worst of times', and so on. It's daring and declarative, with the hypnotic, resonant rhythms of the funeral march: you can hear the beat of the drum as the tumbrils carry the *aristos* to the guillotine. Although it deals in generalities it is atmospheric; the storyteller's voice is clearly heard. We understand at once that in this story we are dealing with individuals caught up in the ineluctable tides of history.It's a great move if you can pull it off. If you're at all uncertain, save the authorial information and observation for a little later and employ it with restraint.

Dialogue

Direct speech is vital to storytelling. When your characters speak, they come to life. The author is not intervening in any way between them and the reader. Waste no time in allowing each character a voice, and making that voice distinctive and particular.

Dialogue has to read like real speech but be cleansed of most of what actually characterises real speech – fluffs, muffs, repetition, failure to complete sentences, and endless 'ums', 'ers', 'you knows' and other interjections which are neither use nor ornament. You can use all these, but extremely sparingly. The purpose of dialogue should be to advance the narrative or the development of character, preferably both at once. If Brian and Daisy are the sort of people who spend the opening five minutes of every exchange discussing the weather and the health of their pets, then *tell* the reader that's what they do. 'After the usual litany of questions and answers concerning the weather and their respective pets . . . ' will do just fine, before getting on to the meat of the conversation. (Of course, if the weather and the pets are pivotal factors in the plot, then that's different.)

Having suggested you make the voice of each character distinct, I must now say – steady as you go with verbal idiosyncrasies. Like all those 'natural' quirks, they are horribly irksome when overdone. A pet phrase may be a wonderful way of earmarking a character, but that person will probably only need to employ it three times in the entire novel to make the point.

If a character has a speech impediment of any kind – a stammer, a stutter, in an inability to pronounce certain letters correctly – tell the reader about it, and indicate it only occasionally in direct speech.

A particular pitfall for the blockbuster writer is the likelihood of speech being set in a far distant time or place. What do you do when your hero is a Knight Templar, or your heroine is working as a surgeon in Papua New Guinea?

Historical

With regard to the first – historical speech – don't fall into the trap of trying to write some kind of special 'old-fashioned' English. 'God-wottery' as it's known, can be absolutely excruciating and will remove, through unintentional humour, all the hard-earned drama and pathos in the rest of your book. 'Thee', 'thou', 'ye', 'zounds!', 'prithee', 'fie!', 'la' and similar archaic expressions have their respective places in the language of the past but have been employed so often as catch-all and usually facetious indicators of history that it's hard to make them work for you in a serious novel. Concentrate instead on using a clear, neutral language, purged of all anachronisms. A friend of mine told me about a film script which she had been sent for consideration. It was about the life of St Francis of Assissi, and contained at one point the startling imprecation: 'You tonsured twit!' I rest my case.

Regional

Regional English poses the same problems. If you've set the scene vividly enough, your reader (who is not a half-wit) will have picked up on the fact that the characters probably speak with the relevant accent or dialect. You only need the very occasional 'Pet' or 'Blimey' (I use these just as examples) to establish that a character is a) Geordie or b) Cockney. Refer to his 'rich West Country burr' or her 'musical Irish lilt' and then let them get on with it. For heaven's sake don't get bogged down into a phonetic representation of the way people speak. A mass of apostrophised glottal stops and distorted vowels will be either comical or such a chore to decode that the reader will be completely turned off.

Foreign

Foreign languages present a special difficulty. Bearing in mind that intelligibility is the *sine qua non* of any narrative, sort out a set of rules for yourself and stick to them. Consistency is vital. If your novel is set in Scandinavia, the chances are that a very high proportion of your characters – even the indigenous ones – will speak English. In Russia it's less likely. Take your tone from your central character. Does she speak the native lingo? If she does, say that she does and then render all exchanges in English. You can occasionally mention that she is actually speaking Russian, and differentiate in the same way when she reverts to English. Introduce an authentic note by learning a handful of key words which will be mentally pronounceable when written in English and use them, in italics, here and there. Don't interpret too literally, but refer obliquely: 'He used the old form of greeting between friends'; or 'She heard the call of the fresh-water-seller on the street outside'. Don't do as the makers of second-rate films were so often wont to do, i.e. give all the foreigners funny accents. If a foreigner is speaking English, suggest the accent as lightly as you can – wrong use of English will be more effective anyway – but if he's speaking his own language, present it as perfect English (without any tell-tale English idioms). And obviously this applies if your central character is foreign in the first place – a Polish aristocrat, a Sioux warrior or whatever.

If your central character is an Englishwoman abroad who doesn't speak the language, then you have a slightly more complex problem on your hands. Be consistent. You are seeing the situation through her eyes. If she doesn't understand then her fear/desire/interest must be conveyed and interpreted in other ways. But if the entire story is to take place in this setting, you have to find a way round it. Either she must learn the language (and not take too long over it) or you must introduce some kind of intermediary who does speak it (this is a bit too cumbersome to be a long-term solution).

Attribution

I'll assume you're confident on matters like attribution (not every remark needs attributing; it's usually the last person named who's speaking. And beware of terms like 'thundered' and 'riposted' – 'said' is usually fine). However, there is one rudimentary logistical matter which merits a mention.

The blockbuster being what it is, you're highly likely to have characters in transit – on the Orient Express, on a horse-drawn sledge, in a red Ferrari, as human flies on a cliff-face. Bear in mind that if they're talking to one another you must from time to time remind the reader of the context. If some dramatic emotional confrontation is being played out in the course of a journey, refer back to your characters' whereabouts from time to time. How has the journey progressed, what's the time of day, the scenery outside the window (where relevant), the temperature, the degree of comfort or discomfort? It's frightfully confusing to read a passage of dialogue which you believe is taking place in downtown Basingstoke, only to discover at the end of it that the characters are driving along the Promenade des Anglais in Nice.

If the dialogue is taking place in one location, then you should also refer to the location here and there. This can also serve as attribution: 'She took a cigarette from the jade box on the desk. "It's over".' or: 'He stood silhouetted against the fading light, "I'm sorry".'

Letting in the light

Dialogue lets light in on the page. No matter how terse your style, how short your paragraphs and crisp your sentences, text appears in solid grey blocks unless dialogue is present. The white spaces on the page and the variety afforded by inverted commas, dashes, exclamation marks and frequent capital letters – all these add to the readability of your novel. If a potential reader is leafing through your book deciding whether or not to buy it, the presence of dialogue will indicate the presence of characters and story. While the characters are speaking, the author is not lecturing or otherwise indulging herself. You know it makes sense because you've been in that choice-making position yourself. If you're anything like me, confronted with several pages of unbroken text you flip over a few more to see when the story proper starts. As a blockbuster-writer you must *always* be able to put yourself in the position of the reader.

Dialogue is breath, movement, sound. It's your characters demonstrating their independent life. While they speak, nothing and no one stands between them and the reader.

There is one more intimate and personal activity, however, where you, the author, do stand between characters and reader, and how much you reveal is entirely up to you.

101

Sex

On this trickiest of subjects the most helpful thing I can do is to refer yet again to the question of confidence. These days it is no longer *de rigueur* to have sex scenes at regular intervals. (My own view is that it never was anyway – no amount of untrammelled coupling can be a substitute for a great story with a strong emotional charge.) But there was a time when that's how it appeared. Sex scenes became more frequent and more eye-boggling than ever before. Now in the chastened and aware nineties there is a spirit of restraint abroad, which has filtered through to popular fiction.

It's odd that the kind of sex which is arguably the most enjoyable and socially acceptable – committed, loving, conversational sex – is the hardest to write about. Brutal sex, comic sex, fumbling pubescent sex and sex for sale are all for some reason easier to deal with in print. Perhaps that's because we can distance ourselves from it, we don't reveal so much of ourselves, so it's not as embarrassing.

There aren't any rules about this, but let me offer one thought for your consideration. You won't write successful (by which I mean effective, erotic, non-cringemaking) sex scenes unless you feel confident and at ease with the writing of them. I am not making an oblique value-judgement here – an awkwardness in writing about sex does not indicate a hormonally-challenged writer. You could be Theydon Bois' answer to Christine Keeler and still be quite unable to translate that experience into print. Go as far as you feel happy with – as far as you feel able to do the subject justice – and then, er, withdraw.

When I wrote *The Flowers of the Field* I was still unsure of my ground in this respect. This was the height of the raunchy 'hot historical' and I felt that without a certain amount of explicit sex my book would sink without trace. Consequently there is a good deal, and some of it is ill-judged. I doubt that in 1913 any well-bred male house guest, no matter how hot his blood, would have had knowledge of his host's teenage daughter on a chaise-longue in the family drawing room after lights out. At any rate, it's there now, for better or worse. I can only thank God I didn't follow the advice of my American editor (the sable coat and diamonds lady) who opined that the heroine's grief on finding her Beloved Enemy dead was unjustifiably intense for a virgin. 'It's just too primal, Sarah,' she boomed over the phone. 'And all on the strength of one little underwater blow-job . . . ' Blow-job? When? She'd read an awful lot more into my lyrical, lakeside picnic scene than I had ever put there.

To this day I don't know whether *The Flowers of the Field* would have sold untold squillions in the States if Thea and Josef had done as my editor suggested and embarked on, shall we say, a 'full-blown' affair. My guess is it would have made no difference.

The emotional content of the relationships is infinitely more important to the story, and to the reader. If the characters are strong, the build-up good, and the narrative tension running high, a relationship will carry its own powerful erotic charge.

Of course if you feel that writing sex scenes is your forte, then play to that strength and make them as good as you possibly can where you feel they're called for. But bear in mind that the novel which is remembered chiefly for the frequency and explicitness of its sex scenes is not necessarily the novel which is most widely read and loved. To be moderate with explicit sex isn't prudish, it's prudent.

With this as with everything else, it's story first.

9

YOU EITHER GOT OR YOU HAVEN'T GOT -

Style

This will certainly be the shortest chapter in the book. Style is one of those areas that every sensible adviser shies away from. Writing about style is like heading a chapter 'The Meaning of Life' or 'The Secrets of the Universe'. But this book isn't a particularly sensible undertaking, so I thought what the heck? The blockbusting mentality does not allow for shying away. I might as well be hanged for a sheep as a lamb.

Style can't be taught. It's the X-factor – the one element in the process whose initiation, culture and nurture is the exclusive province of the individual writer. Style *is* the individual. It's what makes your writing, your novel – and especially your blockbuster – distinct from all others.

What's off the page

A large part of what is generally referred to as style is that authorial 'voice' we spoke about before. If you know that no one can tell the story the way you can, and you embark on your story with this approach, your writing style will evolve naturally from that. In other words, much that is personal style takes place off the page.

Let me tell you a story to illustrate this. When my second novel *A Flower That's Free* came out – following three years of inertia-panic confronting writer's block – I was booked to speak at a prestigious literary dinner in Harrogate. My fellow speakers were a witty Yorkshire woman who'd had a great local success with her autobiographical account of running an organic farm singlehanded, and the doyen of *Mastermind*, the thinking woman's fancy, Magnus

Magnusson. I should have realised as soon as I received these details in the post that I was probably on a hiding to nothing and that a becoming diffidence might be my best route to the hearts of my audience.

I should have realised, but I didn't. On the contrary I got all excitable at the thought of the competition and decided I was going to knock the socks off everyone present.

Dinner ended, speeches loomed. They'd put me on second, where the first five minutes of my brief speech would bob in the slipstream of the audience's riotous approval of the lady farmer, and the second five minutes languish becalmed in their rapt anticipation of Magnus. Undaunted, I went for it. I gave them gags, anecdotes and *aperçus* in full measure – more than they could possibly have asked or hoped for at the relatively modest ticket price. The lady farmer chuckled indulgently. Magnus smiled in that twinkly, reflective way of his. They could afford to be nice, because I died . . .

Afterwards I sat alone and ignored at my signing table flanked by the bravely smiling representatives of my publisher. From the tables on either side, long queues of customers wound out of the room and down the stairs, their wads and cheques at the ready. Magnus and the lady farmer were getting writer's cramp. I was mortified. What in heaven's name had I done wrong? I'd been witty and assertive and self-assured, I'd spoken to time and alluded to the beauties of Harrogate and the warmth and wit of Yorkshire people. I'd assiduously promoted my new book, out that very day in all good bookshops. And yet I was dead in the water.

I was just about ready to throw in the towel and slink off to my room, when a woman came up to my table. She carried freshly signed copies of both my fellow speakers' books. But she looked kindly, and I was desperate. I responded to her like a wanderer in the desert spotting a test-tube full of pond water. I picked up a copy of my novel! I took the cap off my pen!

'I'm sorry, my dear,' she said, laying a restraining hand on my arm, 'I can't afford any more books.' My face fell. 'Don't worry, I'll get it out of the library,' she added, and then leaned forward confidingly and squeezed my hand. 'I know I'll enjoy it – I liked your *mind.*'

105

I went up to bed consoled. She'd given me approval in the one area where every writer wants it. A novel is so personal, and contains such a huge emotional investment, that each reaction is a reaction to us as individuals. That nice Yorkshire lady helped me forget the 199 other people there that night – she liked my style!

I can tell this story with a certain smugness now, because at the end of the following week *A Flower That's Free* went straight into the bestseller list at Number 2. But it does help to think of style in its wider sense.

Part of the whole

Personal style – in dress, appearance, manner – is not artificially imposed, it evolves. The most stylish people are those whose style seems to be an absolutely natural, organic extension of the people they are – it's impossible to imagine them any other way. In the same way literary style should grow out of the writer's experience, her reading, her character and her feelings towards what she is writing. Your style, once you have it, will to some extent adapt itself to your material (the style you use for a comic contemporary novel will not be precisely the same as that you use for an historical blockbuster), but its essence – the part that is your mind – will be a constant, recognisable factor.

I'm a great admirer of Margaret Forster. She writes wonderfully, and distinctively, whatever her subject matter. Her novel *Lady's Maid* concerns the love affair, marriage and elopement of Elizabeth Barrett and Robert Browning as seen through the eyes of Elizabeth's maid. The tone and language are those of a Victorian working-class woman. They're so well judged, and the novel so well constructed, that it's hard to believe one isn't reading an autobiography. In *Have the Men Had Enough?* Margaret Forster deals with the painful domestic and emotional issues confronted by a family when an elderly relative has Alzheimer's. By her own admission, the novel *is* as close to reality as any novel she's written; she began it soon after her own mother-in-law's death. The two books could not be more different in subject and structure. And yet both are identifiably and inimitably Margaret Forster. They have her stamp – her style.

So that's the mystical part – and it's by far the most important. There remain several practical considerations.

Is less more?

I've already hinted that it is. And speaking as someone who has an inbuilt tendency to overwrite, I'm darn sure that less is more. After all, writers are in the business of communication, and communication to be effective must be clear and direct. Deliberately to distort what you write for effect goes against the principle of clear communication. On the other hand, we want to create special effects, the pyrotechnics of writing are undeniably fun.

The blockbuster, too, is something of a special case. It should have a quality of richness, of being stuffed as full of good things as a Christmas pudding. That quality of being richly satisfying is one of its prevailing characteristics. I said earlier that your style will adapt to your circumstances, and in a blockbuster you can allow yourself some room for manoeuvre. Descriptive detail and occasional digressions are fine in this context provided you never let the narrative tension slacken. The best way of making description 'relevant' and lively is to present it from one character's point of view. Who is seeing this particular scene, or experiencing these events? What is their frame of mind? What do they expect, hope for, fear? The answers to these questions will colour your description, so that it becomes part of your narrative, and not an effusion designed to show off your knowledge and vocabulary. There is a fine line between not short-changing the reader and self-indulgent over-writing. Provided you can always feel the pull, you should be able to tread that line successfully.

What I have to say next may appear rudimentary, but it's impossible to avoid in any discussion of style.

Adjectives

Adjectives have got themselves a bad name, which is a shame because they are a valuable part of speech with a proud history.

Their fall from grace has to do with their widespread misuse. I seem to remember that at school my otherwise wonderful English teacher enthusiastically fostered the adjectival group of three: 'lonely, bleak, desolate', 'tall, dark, handsome', 'blonde, blue-eyed, beautiful', and so on. Much was made of the pleasing cadences of these groups, of the cumulative effect of piling one adjective upon another, when actually the opposite is true. One well-chosen adjective used in the right place in the right way is infinitely more telling than clusters, in which the words have a tendency to cancel each other out.

Here's a short descriptive passage:

> That day the peddler arrived in town. It was noon. The heat pressed on the rooftops and the dogs, sprawled in the shade, had no energy to bark, though their hackles rose.
>
> The peddler wore a cloak the colour of blood; its corners dragged in the dust. He'd pulled the brim of his hat down to shield his face from the glare, and from the curiosity of the locals. From every part of him there hung his wares: saucepans, spoons, necklaces, ribbons, toys, tools and knives. As he strode past the cottages the jangling of these objects, like a prisoner's chains, was the only sound in the silence.
>
> In his hand the peddler held a staff. But it was at the hand itself that the people stared: it was a hand like an animal's paw, stunted by leprosy. Doors closed, children were snatched away. Only the dogs remained in the street. People preferred to huddle in darkness and safety than to share the sunlight with a leper.

These short paragraphs tell us a lot about the atmosphere, period and sinister persona of the peddler. What's important is that they do so without the use of adjectives. While there's nothing inherently good about leaving adjectives out, it's useful to observe and understand the effect of doing so. To describe without using 'describing words' you have to *show*. It follows that your description will be more active and contain more lively and apposite metaphor. 'A cloak the colour of blood' tells us more about the cloak and the man wearing it than 'a red cloak'. Against that, it uses more words. Instead of describing the quality of the heat, I've had to show its effects – the dogs lying motionless in the shade, people sheltering behind their shutters, and so on. It's a filmic technique, 'shot' piled on shot to create an effect. If one always wrote like this, it would sooner or later seem awkward and circuitous, but to be aware of the differences is to add another tool to the tool-kit.

A blockbuster novel should describe things fully. Since you're taking the reader into another world it follows that you should paint as vivid a picture of that world as possible. And yet descriptive padding for its own sake is dull – so how do we reconcile these two factors?

By having *more to say*. If you want to describe the inside of a grand ocean liner, you need enough material at your disposal to be able to select what's genuinely riveting, and germane to your plot and characters, and to leave out what is simply information for information's sake.

For instance, if in the description of your ocean liner the main viewpoint is that of a small child, she is going to be impressed by the scale, strangeness and grandeur of her surroundings – the staterooms, the beds, the bathrooms, the lounges, the food, the appearance and manner of other passengers, crew and stewards.

If the viewpoint is that of a business tycoon, accustomed to travel in style, he will accept most of what he sees as 'given' – in other words, you can mention it, but in passing – and will home in on what is exceptional, either good or bad. His satisfaction and/or criticisms will tell the reader a lot about the ship and the character. Point of view again, here as it affects your style.

What follows is an excerpt from *The Flowers of the Field*, a description of London during the Armistice celebrations of 1918, as seen by Maurice, a conscientious objector:

He cut through to Cambridge Circus, knowing it was out of his way but hoping to hop on a bus in the Charing Cross Road, but the only bus he saw was piled high with tier upon tier of young men, filling the interior and clinging to the outside. Some were in uniform, others in civvies, some in a mixture of the two. Their arms waved and fluttered from the sides of the bus so that it resembled a gigantic moving sea anemone with a thousand fronds.

He utterly abandoned the idea of any form of transport and resigned himself, rather fearfully, to reaching the Buchanan on foot. He was irrevocably commited to the journey now and the knowledge made him panicky. The exuberant crowd seemed a howling, predatory mob, he mistrusted them. The atmosphere abroad in the streets resembled nothing so much as that which had so sickened him at the outbreak of war. These normally sane people, the survivors of the war and inheritors of the peace, who for four bitter years had been so courageous and full of sense and fortitude, had now gone mad. They were not celebrating peace, but war and the winning of it, demonstrating with a lunatic vivacity that it had all been worth it. They were conquerors!

In Trafalgar Square it was worse than ever. The place where he had sat with Primmy, both water and wall, was covered by a crowd so dense it resembled a field of corn, the surface riffled by the swaying of heads as they sang. The concourse was made up of several different factions, each singing its own song at full blast, oblivious to competition. The resulting dissonant roar reminded Maurice of the sound of the guns, heard far-off from the Soot Street camp. At the foot of Nelson's Column some Canadians had lit a gigantic bonfire. Its shivering coppery light illuminated the aloof faces of the stone lions, and sparks flew up into the dark sky like scarlet stars.

On the steps of St Martin's in the Fields an elderly woman leaned up against the wall. At first he thought she was drunk, but on closer inspection it was plain she had the 'flu. She was clammy and feverish and her face had a darkened appearance, symptom of the pulmonary complications which had made this second outbreak so lethal. Thousands had died, it was like the final kick in the side of an already fallen man. Maurice shouted in her ear, but she was too far gone to hear. He considered taking her to Charing Cross, but she would have been far too heavy to carry and the street was packed. She looked ominously close to death.

After that, he felt markedly worse. His own mild chesty cold seemed to take on a new dimension. Not that he seriously thought he would get the 'flu, he imagined that his bout in the summer had afforded him some kind of immunization, but nonetheless . . . He buttoned the top of his jacket and pushed his hands deep into his pockets. Thea had found his coat, and given it to him, but he was hopelessly forgetful, and always walked out in whatever he had on.

Tortuously, he circumnavigated Trafalgar Square. All the grinning faces, the noise, the sparks, the buffeting, began to induce a kind of delirium in Maurice. He was miserable and frankly terrified. The old feeling of his physical vulnerability overcame him. Why, they could literally trample him underfoot and never notice! Worried that his spectacles would be broken he took them off and put them in his jacket pocket, holding them there in his hand. The yelling grimacing faces receded, became amorphous, reeling blobs of colour. Using the comforting bulk of the National Gallery on his right as a lode star, he staggered along in the direction of Lower Regent Street.

Set piece or purple passage?

The one is perfectly acceptable, the second is strenuously to be avoided. The trouble is, they're hard to tell apart when you write them yourself. When you come across them in the pages of some-one else's novel they're instantly identifiable.

The set piece is a scene in which an important narrative step is taken, at one time and in one place. The players are all present, the setting is probably of some interest in itself, and the action proceeds continuously, almost like a complete short story within the novel. There is a scene near the beginning of *The Flowers of the Field* in which the whole Tennant family convenes in the hall to decorate the Christmas tree. This is a set piece: a good way of introducing all the characters and their relationships to one another. Tensions, loyalties, resentments and rivalries are shown in a confined domestic context before the characters step out on to a wider stage.

I'm not going to confess to any purple passages, nor am I going to risk lynching by pointing them out in the work of other people, but we've all encountered them, or indulged in them, at one time or another. From a reader's point of view they generally evoke the response 'Crikey!' – prior to a swift turning of the page. A purple passage is self-indulgent, the author is speaking to no one but herself. It's self-serving in another way too, because it fills space to no useful dramatic or narrative end. If you find yourself wondering how best to describe the exact quality of sunlight playing on the surface of a lake – you're probably heading for a purple passage.

Tics

Yet again I find myself in the position of seeming to hedge my bets, which only goes to show what a complex business writing is.

I've said that style is the X-factor – the part of the novel which is identifiably individual and unique. But I'd be failing in my duty if I didn't warn you about tics – those words, phrases and verbal mannerisms which (just as in everyday behaviour) you are not aware of, and therefore tend to replicate over and over again to the inevitable annoyance of the reader. Picture yourself sitting next to someone on a bus. She brushes aside a lock of hair. The gesture is charming. She does it again. And again. You begin to count the times. It starts to get on your nerves. In fact, it's a maddening habit! You need a way of writing that is characteristic and fresh, without giving a free rein to all your little habits.

I have a tendency to overdo all those qualifying and modifying words – 'rather', 'quite', 'sort of', 'slightly', 'kind of' – which I suppose betrays a 'kind of' anxiety about committing myself completely to a given perspective. Or it may be that English disease of inherent irony – the double agenda. Whatever the cause, it's all dead wood clogging up the story and making things less clear. The words are fine when they're to be taken literally, but not where they fudge the issue.

Being aware of these tics is two-thirds of the battle, but the trouble with this sort of thing is often that you are *not* aware of it, or you wouldn't keep doing it. A good copy-editor will pick up tics and point them out to you – be guided by her. In a blockbuster novel there is likely to be more space for a tic to be repeated – more 'occasions of sin' – and it's that much more likely to be irritating.

Another of my personal tics is over-punctuation. That old English teacher of mine, along with her adjectival groups of three, dinned into me that 'punctuation is the good manners of writing' – something I still firmly believe to be true. A strategically placed comma or semi-colon can fine-tune the meaning of a sentence. But a series of short statements, unpunctuated but for full stops, can be equally effective. My trouble is I love all of it – commas, colons, dots, dashes, exclamation marks, the works. And the fashion has changed – the comma in particular is in retreat. Where dialogue is concerned, novels seem to have absorbed some of the characteristics of the television script, where the words are left more or less unadorned, waiting for the actor – or in this case the reader – to colour them by their reading. I don't 'see' my excessive punctuation until I get the novel in proof form. This is the first time one actually sees one's book as a book, and the salutary effect is to make what's different about it jump off the page. This can be pleasing or, in the case of my punctuation, dismaying. My printed pages bristle with fussy little marks. The punctuation is not incorrect, but its over-use appears 'nannying' – giving too many instructions as though the reader is slow or simple-minded.

Which brings me to something else.

Space for the imagination

Just now I mentioned the desirability in scripted dialogue of leaving room for the actor to work. A television script is like dehydrated soup – all the ingredients and flavours are there but rendered-down, waiting for the contributions of numerous other people, and the actors in particular, to reconstitute the meal and serve it up in all its delicious completeness.

The novel, especially the blockbuster novel, is not an invitation to collaborate like the television script, but a complete form. You, the novelist, are in charge. Story, plot, characters, dialogue and description are all down to you. But don't forget to flatter and involve the reader. A really enjoyable story is a collusion between writer and reader. Reading is an exercise of the imagination just as writing is. A description which stimulates and provokes the imagination and leaves room for it to operate is far more effective than one which overloads the reader with so much information it's all she can do to digest it, and she's left with nowhere to go. This doesn't mean short-changing the reader – be bold about showing the drama as your narrative unfolds, but remember always to leave a little 'air' around what you write, so that your reader can add something of her own.

Breaking the veil

Don't be pompous. 'Author-talking' is a trap lying in wait for the unwary novelist, especially one who is attempting a blockbuster. In trying to exude confidence and passion, and to ensure a masterful narrative overview, you may be tempted to make authorial interventions. You may not actually begin a passage 'Dear reader,' but you might as well – you are lecturing the reader. Be cautious about devices such as 'He was not to know that . . . ' and 'So what was Uncle David doing all this time . . . ?' Don't kid yourself that

113

these interventions are the same thing as the writer/reader collusion we talked about earlier. They're not. This is not an organic process but a thumping great impertinence which the reader will find irritating and intrusive.

You are writing fiction. Fiction is an illusion. The moment you speak as the author you rupture the illusion, and upset the delicate balance between storyteller and story-reader. The only place where this is acceptable is in first-person narrative where the narrator is also a character in her own right.

If you are tempted to take the reader aside, remember that this is the most overt kind of 'Tell' storytelling, so it's clumsy on several levels.

'Murder your darlings'

I started out by saying that you can't impose a style on your writing – it will evolve. The chances are that the seeds of your style were there in the first serious piece you ever wrote (I mean serious in intent, not lacking in humour). A read-round at any writers' group, even where all present are amateurs or beginners, will reveal as many different styles as there are people in the room. Whether they're effective as yet is neither here nor there. What each writer has to learn is how to know and play to her strengths and recognise and be ruthless with her weaknesses.

We all need help. I'm very afraid that most of us don't know what we do best, and certainly aren't aware of quite how bad we can get. Force yourself to look back at what you've written and remove everything that is a fudge, a repetition, or an irrelevancy. In the long term you may aspire to a style that is more elaborate, but you can do no better than to begin with absolute simplicity, clarity and directness. There is no such thing as under-writing in terms of style (though there is in terms of content). But over-writing is the besetting sin of most of us, and the remedy for the purple passage is best summed-up by Samuel Johnson:

'Read over your compositions, and where ever you meet with a passage which you think is particularly fine, strike it out.'

10

MOVING ON

The research for, and writing of, a blockbuster could easily take two years – possibly more. It will become a way of life. The very effect you want to have on your reader – i.e. 'I never want this book to end!' – can be a snare for the author. You must know when the story is complete.

Ending

Knowing how your blockbuster ends will not detract from, but add to, the excitement you feel in writing it, and increase the narrative tension that makes your reader turn the page. But 'how' can be less of an issue than 'when'. In the early stages, or about halfway through your novel, you may experience a long dark coffee-break of the soul. I commented on this once when we had some friends round for supper. 'I feel so bleak,' I droned pretentiously. 'I'm too far from the beginning to give up, but so far from the end that's all I want to do!' My friends' faces were studies in earnest sympathy, but from a distant corner of the room a voice piped up: 'How do you think the reader feels?' Yes.

Ripeness is all, with endings. You mustn't appear to accelerate indecently into the home straight, like an old pony my daughter once had, who shuffled on the way out and was unrestrainable on the way back. You must resolve the different strands of the story, complete the narrative arc (often with a small lilt or upward curve at the end), conclude the journey of your central characters, but you must do all this without presenting your reader with a series of false crests, which may exhaust her patience and her concentration. I don't mean twists, they're fine. I mean the sort of narrative scab-picking and after-thoughts which add nothing to the story. You will probably dream of the day you write those words 'The End', but as they draw closer, so you start to put the brakes on, for reasons we've mentioned. After all, when you've written them, what then? Think of your original concept and stay true to it.

This is when a written outline comes into its own. It's a compass, a talisman, a road map. It will help you reach a fully rounded ending at the right time and place.

Perversely, one thing you may want to do when you get to the end is go back to the beginning. The journey that you've travelled with your characters will have effected changes in you as well as them, and several hundred pages on, you may well see your opening chapter in a new light. Knowing what you now know, could there be a better or more dramatic way of doing things? You may wish to show a new perspective on certain characters and events, or give them a different emphasis. Now that the pressure simply to finish is off, you have time to make adjustments.

Revision

There are no rules about how many drafts or how much revision you should do. It's like the work schedule – don't be fazed by other people's methods. Some people do umpteen drafts, others one. I can only do two before I feel the need for some feedback from someone else. Basically I've seen enough of the book then and want a break from it: if anything else is going to be done to it, it has to have originated elsewhere. I've temporarily shot my bolt.

The criterion for revision is simple: you want your book to be as wonderful as it can be. This means the story needs to be riveting, without gaps or inconsistencies; the characters must be totally credible, and leap off the page; the writing must be clear, vivid, and not repetitive or self-indulgent; and the facts must be correct.

The facts are the most straightforward thing to get right. They'll probably be right in the first place, and it's a fairly simple job to double-check those you're not quite sure of. Don't neglect the ones you *are* sure of – sod's law dictates that certainty rides before a fall. I was absolutely sure that 'The Lambeth Walk' was a music-hall song, and I used it in *The Flowers of the Field*, sung by a group of Londoners as they celebrated in the streets of London on Armistice Night. My agent thought the same thing – so, alas, did my editor, my copy-editor and the typesetter. It went through on the nod. We were all wrong. The song was written in 1936 by Noel Gay for his musical *Me and My Girl*. The people who did know were my readers who wrote in by the sackful pointing out my error. What could I do but eat crow? The moral of the story is check everything, whether or not you're in any doubt.

With regard to the other and more important issues, try to look at your book as a reader would. Don't suppose the reader to be more stupid, less imaginative or slower than you – the only difference is that she didn't write the book. Ask yourself on every page – would I want to put the book down at this point? Is this boring? Is it necessary? Have I said it in the best way possible? This doesn't mean you have to make everything more 'sensational'. It just has to be – well – sensational. Quiet, thoughtful scenes must be every bit as compelling as those which are more obviously dramatic. Bear in mind the huge advantage of Show over Tell. Is there some important scene which you've sidestepped or simply reported? And conversely, are there areas where you've wasted space on what is no more than 'recitative'? Are times and places clear, especially if you've backtracked or used direct-action flashbacks? *You* know the exact moment when something's happening, but might a reader be confused?

Now is the moment to enjoy yourself changing the opening and closing sentences so that they are unforgettably wonderful.

Presentation

I know, I know, you already know all about this. You've been told a hundred times about numbering, and double-spacing, and indentation, and margins and getting a really sharp print-out. You know about keeping a copy, and sending postage and doing a word-count. And just as well you do, because they're all essential.

But a long typescript presents special problems. I was recently chair of the judges for a literary prize, and had to read a huge number of first-time novels (well, a huge number for me, though any agent or editor would call it child's play). I found rather to my embarrassment that I had to discriminate positively, or at least mentally compensate, for those which were still in typescript. They can be so bally awkward to read! And the longer they are the more awkward they are. In fact it was really only convenient to sit at a table or a desk, when what I wanted to do was lie on the sofa with my feet up. Nor did it follow that the bound typescripts were any better. Nothing's more devilish to read than several hundred sheets joined together in a folder – they take on a life of their own, springing back at you, flopping over, with a deep gully down the middle that makes reading the first three words on every line like trying to discern the maker's mark on the bottom of a grandfather clock.

My agent agreed, glad that I was taking on board this small practical lesson. She said that as far as she was concerned the simplest, most convenient way to present a long typescript was in an A4 box – the one that your paper came out of in the first place. The lid can be placed alongside and the pages, once read, placed face down in the lid. When the book's finished, the two halves can be reunited and Bob's your uncle. Having just struggled for several weeks with sheaves of type with a life of their own, either fighting free of bindings or fluttering and drifting all over the floor, I could appreciate the perfect simplicity of it. The snag is that most A4 paper no longer comes in a box but in a heavy-duty paper wrapping. I have to scour the local offices and retail outlets to find the right boxes, but the glow of virtue when I bring home the bacon makes it worth it.

Fear!

So now, finally, you have to find the courage to send your block-buster on the next stage of its journey, alone. Courage is certainly not too strong a word. The rash daring that prompted you to begin a blockbuster is nothing to the cool head and steady nerve you'll need to part with it.

A number of factors contribute to this anxiety:

- A natural disinclination to separate from what has been your *raison d'être* for a sizeable chunk of time.
- Fear of criticism.
- Fear of rejection.
- Fear of failure (not the same thing).
- The question: 'What about Mother?'

So what *about* Mother?

This may not be the most important factor on the list, but it's a perfectly serious worry with a lot of authors, especially when they go for broke. Writing a big novel with a strong emotional content leaves you in a very exposed position. Your attitudes, feelings and opinions will inform what you write – and if the passions in your story run high there is a strong possibility that you will shock, even without using shocking material. No one in their right mind sets out deliberately to libel, defame or grossly offend in print, but anything short of that is fair game. And being the writer you are, you'll make full use of it. The queasiness sets in when you realise your kith, kin and the nice people next door are going to read this book.

Two stories. Following publication of *The Flowers of the Field* my father was out on the golf course at the East Devon club where he'd been a member for something like forty years. While rummaging in the rough for a mislaid ball he encountered a fellow member, a bishop, also rummaging. The exchange went something like this:

MY FATHER: Morning, Bishop.
BISHOP: Morning, Tony.
MY FATHER: Nice day for it.
BISHOP: Indeed it is . . . (PREGNANT PAUSE) I say, Tony – your daughter certainly calls a spade a spade!

My father abandoned his search.

My next book, *A Flower That's Free*, also contains several graphic scenes, both of wartime atrocities and sexual obsession. An elderly friend whose wife was in a nursing home told my parents that he was well into the book and it was bringing back many memories. 'Joyce and I are enjoying it together,' he added. 'I'm reading it aloud to her in the residents' lounge.' Added to her many afflictions, poor Joyce was very deaf. We wondered what the other residents were making of it . . .

Hot Breath, though not a blockbuster, was a wonderful profile-raiser, partly because it was so obviously open to the charge of being autobiographical. I say nothing. But I remember my mother ringing me up and saying: '*I* laughed like a drain, darling, but I think there may be one or two people down here *passing by on the other side.*'

You can't afford to be restricted or put off your stroke by what others may think. It's quite possible that some of them may be shocked, or piqued, or astonished some of the time, but they will also be gobsmacked with admiration and basking in reflected glory. Give them credit for being serious readers as well as people who happen to know you. They'll get over it, and so will you.

And so back to the start of the list.

Not wanting to part with it

This is perfectly natural. After all, while it's with you, lying on your desk or illuminated on the screen, all things are still possible. My Finnish publisher said something astute: 'While a book is being written it's like a bird, flying around, going where it wants, as free as air. Once it's in print it becomes a stuffed bird in a glass case . . . '

In other words, the book, once published, is in a static state. Your story's life transfers from your head, heart and imagination to the limbo of the bookshelf, and then to the head, heart and imagination of the reader. No matter how many second or third thoughts you have, no matter what regrets or sudden brainwaves, or flashes of imagination, it's too late now. Or too late for that particular book. But writing, like life, is a learning experience, and if there are lessons to be learned you'll put them into practice next time around. Won't you?

Fear of criticism

Conquer it at all costs. Nobody *likes* criticism, but actually to avoid it, especially if you aspire to write a bestselling novel, is sheer pig-headed folly. Remember the stuffed bird – once the novel is, as we hope, published, there is no course open to the self-critical author but a ritual burning. Now is the time to get it right, and anything or anyone who can help you do that is to be welcomed.

To this end, don't be tempted to ask the opinion of a friend, relation or partner (especially partner) unless the person concerned is a hugely distinguished writer/publisher/literary agent, and even then I'd counsel against it, not because these people won't criticise, but because whatever they do you'll take it personally. If they say 'It's wonderful!', and offer nothing but praise you'll be quite understandably sceptical. If they criticise, you won't be able to sift out what's useful, because your feelings will be hurt – yes, they will – and you may also hold against them the one thing they can't help: that they're not experts. Feedback from friends and relations is an emotional and professional minefield. Time enough for their response when the novel is safely stowed between hard covers. For now, what you need is the reaction of a sound, dispassionate professional.

If you already have a good agent, or are able to get yourself one, then she's your first port of call. She'll know your writing, and you, and whatever she says should be taken extremely seriously. After all, both she and your publisher are on the same side as you – they want your book to work, and to work BIG. I'm thrice blessed in having as an agent Carol Smith, who is not only a first-class businesswoman, but a fund of creative advice, and now a bestselling novelist in her own right, so she has the benefit of complementary perspectives. Admittedly we've been together for twenty-five years (that shocked me when I worked it out, I can tell you), so we're now close friends and she knows my writing, my emotional make-up, my strengths, weaknesses and idiosyncrasies as well as I do myself. But she it was whose professional matchmaking and nose for a good idea launched me on *The Flowers of the Field* when I was a completely unknown short-story writer with no track record as a novelist. Back then, although I longed to write a novel I had no sense of my own identity as a writer. The fledgling voice in my short stories was almost stifled by the demands of writing for a strict market. What I needed was what the ad-men call the 'permission' to try something I would probably never have had the audacity to attempt on my own. All through my writing career Carol has been the constant, keeping me up to the mark, supporting me in many of my wilder flights, restraining me from committing professional suicide on more than one occasion, helping me play to my strengths, and standing between me and the harsh realities of contracts, deals, clauses and options.

None of this means we don't have spats. Long before *The Flowers of the Field* was published I remember dissolving embarrassingly on the phone to Carol because she had given yet another of my 'ground-breaking' ideas the bum's rush. Blubbing uncontrollably, awash with self-pity and wounded pride, I chucked everything at the hapless Carol, from 'You don't understand!' to 'Other people get away with it!' Why she didn't let me go there and then I'll never know. I was emphatically not the brightest literary prospect in town, and not just an unfocused mediocrity but a whining unfocused mediocrity. However, to her eternal credit and my immense good fortune, Carol hung in there.

She is still my keenest critic, and I still take criticism badly, both from her and my editor. But I do take it. I've learned what I have to do to cultivate a balanced approach.

Coping

For a start, I now accept that I lack judgement in certain areas and that there's no point, to employ an old adage, in having a dog and barking yourself. What a good agent or editor has is overview – she reads not only your work, but the work of numerous other writers. She has a keen appreciation not only of the market place, but of where any particular author stands in relation to others –

her identity. Though there is an element of subjectivity in any intelligent response, she is not being merely subjective or whimsical when she says that she doesn't care for the ending/beginning/ prison scene/heroine. The reservations she feels are in her water, the product of her special talent, her experience, and her knowledge of you as a writer. She doesn't voice them lightly. She is not criticising simply for something to do, or to keep you in some way 'on your toes' – why on earth should she do that? She wants you to feel secure and confident, and your book (particularly if it's a potential blockbuster) to be as good as it possibly can, just as you do. That doesn't mean she's always right, but it does mean you should take everything she says seriously.

My advice, as a notoriously poor criticisee, is: don't act in haste, or in heat. No matter what it costs you in terms of self-control, listen to the criticism, or read it, and then end the call politely, set the letter aside, dash out into the garden and scream blue murder. Do whatever needs doing to let off steam. Grab a friend – this is when friends really are useful – and dump it all on her. Tell her how you have to deal with people who don't understand you, how you're being asked to compromise your artistic soul, how you will *not*, no way, how incredible it is that these people don't *see* how crass their God-awful suggestions are! Your friend, given a glass of wine and a following wind, will listen like the good sort she is. Anyway, what does she care? The *dramatis personae* are all strangers to her. She can afford to look sage and sympathetic as you give her all this baloney. It's what she's there for. She may even feel flattered to be included in the creative process, though that's unlikely if she's ever been subjected to this kind of thing before.

On the principle that a trouble shared is a trouble if not halved at least substantially shrunk, you'll feel better after this tirade. It's taken a lot of the heat out of the subject. The next stage is to let some distance develop between you and the unreasonable and insensitive comments of your editor. Take a break – I don't mean an hour, I mean several days. Pay no attention to the work in question, and definitely pay no never-mind to those hurtful and offensive criticisms. Do something else. See people, buy clothes, build a rumpus room, walk the Pennine Way. When the outrage has subsided, go back to it. Read or reconsider the criticisms, and then read over your typescript in the light of them. Being the intelligent person and the talented writer that you are, you will in all probability begin to see the sense in much of what has been suggested. It may even seem quite interesting and rewarding to try and put the suggestions into effect in a way that will enhance your novel and which you will find satisfying. And you don't have to agree to, or with, everything. Look dispassionately at what you've written. You are still the author. You're in charge. You bear a heavy responsibility, now's your chance to take some pride and pleasure in discharging that responsibility.

The unkindest cut

Editorial advice often involves cutting. Most authors have a big problem letting stuff go. Especially when it's not necessarily bad material – it may even be good, but surplus to requirements, not wanted on voyage. After all, you wrote such-and-such because you believed in it. It's awfully hard to jettison what is 'perfectly good' – but remember the last time you cleared out the wardrobe/ loft/china cupboard? Remember the way you hummed and hawed over that Coalport meat dish that belonged to Auntie Avis, or the tapestry firescreen with the uneven feet, or the white cotton boiler-suit in which you always looked like the side of a house? 'Perfectly good' is a weasel phrase. It almost always describes an article which, the instant you chuck it out, will be consigned to oblivion, never to enter your thoughts again.

So with the passages that need to be cut. And if they are perfectly good, but not needed on this particular voyage, maybe there will be a place for them in some future novel. Those felicitous phrases, those telling idioms, those witty and insouciant gracenotes – bin them but don't empty the bin. I'd be prepared to bet that once the next novel's under way you'll empty the bin without even bothering to check what's in it, and what's more you won't care.

Going round in circles

A quick word about writers' circles. If you belong to one, try to see it as a support system, of which you make use – not as an end in itself. Of their very nature such groups comprise mostly keen amateur writers, or writers of relatively limited experience. You are probably one such yourself. Don't fall into the trap of writing to please the circle. The comments and criticisms of fellow-members (if you invite them) should be taken on board, but beware the trap of 'cosiness'. You are writing a blockbuster in order to fly the nest – to render the role of the writers' circle redundant.

And if you think I'm being superior, I'm president and currently secretary of my local writers' circle.

Fear of rejection

Let me put it this way – if a professional is offering criticism and advice, they think your novel's viable. They may actually be mad for it, and want it to be *even* better than it already is. You'll be able to handle the criticism much more calmly and constructively if you remind yourself that things could be much worse – you could have been rejected.

Rejection is awful.

There's no way of sugaring the pill, or softening the blow. To be told 'Thanks but no thanks' is to have a knife plunged into your heart and then jiggled about a bit for good measure. It hurts. If you think you respond badly to criticism, it's nothing to the wobbler you'll toss when rejected. Because of course it is you, personally, who are being turned down – not just your story, style and characters, but the way you think and feel. The business of writing a novel has much in common with taking all your clothes off and jogging round the hard shoulder of the M25. It's brave but barmy – and it puts you in a very exposed position.

If, when you've done all that work and poured out all that thought and feeling on to the page, some heartless functionary with an expense account and a safe job tells you it's not up to scratch, you are going to despair. You'll hate the person who did it

125

to you and you'll hate yourself. Every book on the shelf at home and in your local bookshop will appear inferior to the one that's been rejected. The injustice, arbitrariness and cruelty of what's happened will be beyond belief.

Except that it's not. It's all too believable, and common. In fact, it's the norm. Hundreds of thousands of books are published each year, but for every one of those there are another six which wing their way back to their devastated authors after one reading, and sometimes not even that. You have not been singled out for shoddy treatment. You are in the majority.

I accept that knowing this may make things worse. Perhaps it's better to feel that one is unique – that some particularly outrageous sally of yours was just too audacious for that jobsworth publisher to handle. This is rarely the case. The fact is that quality, whether crowd-pleasing middle-of the-road or daringly avant-garde, will out. You will be judged according to your lights, like with like. It's a waste of time glaring through a blur of furious tears at the 100-page Western on the station bookstall and asking yourself how this got published while your book didn't. You weren't trying to write a 100-page western but a 500-page blockbuster. Simply accept that as far as that editor was concerned, you weren't quite good enough.

Nil desperandum

There's no need to jettison hope completely, however. There is a strong element of subjectivity in all this. A good editor is good because she is individual and intuitive, and has clearly defined and cultivated tastes. *She* may not like your novel, but somewhere out there there may be another editor, equally individual, in whom, with all its manifold shortcomings, it will strike a chord. (She it is who may pay you the compliment of offering criticism and advice). Publishing lore abounds with tales of novels that did the rounds of every office in town before finally being picked up and published and becoming blockbusters, their authors household names.

So don't despair too early. Another function of a good agent is that she will absorb the blows for you – it is she who will receive the rejections, and she may not even choose to tell you about them until she has exhausted all the options, and gleaned whatever encouraging comments she can. It's worse if you personally have to keep picking yourself up, dusting yourself down, and recycling the Jiffy-bag. Having a good agent will reduce the risk of rejection simply because the editor reading your manuscript will see that it has already passed through one selection process. Also, reputable agents, publishers and editors know each other and can often negotiate something which leaves room for hope where none might otherwise exist. What many rejected authors see bitterly as the 'closed shop' of publishing can often work in your favour. 'If so-and-so really liked this, might there be something I'm missing . . . ?'

Probably the most useful tip I can give you about coping with rejection is to reduce its importance in your life – and the way to do this is to start work on something else. To put your life on hold is to allow the possibility of rejection to loom too large. Take a breather, of course, but then begin to think about your next book. Start to plan, to make notes, to do research, to formulate ideas, to enjoy starting the process over again. That way, if rejection does slip through the letter box, you can raise two fingers to it, because you're a professional writer who's on to something else.

Fear of failure

This is different again. Rejection may be seen as a failure of sorts, but you can comfort yourself that those responsible are only fallible individuals – and that their lack of enthusiasm is subjective, and ultimately their loss. (I'm not recommending you think like this, simply giving you permission if you want to.)

The failure which is harder to take is when the book is published, but doesn't come up to expectation. At your present stage, you may regard this as a mere bagatelle, because publication is the goal. But it's not, is it? It's the first hurdle, certainly, but you want to write a *blockbuster* – and that means a book that sells hugely and widely. What if your novel's published but in spite of the publisher's best efforts in terms of publicity and promotion, it simply doesn't sell in sufficient numbers?

Here there can be no dodging the issue. You may have done everything right, and the publisher clearly also took that view, but the public didn't agree. You have failed to set them alight. Some of them bought it, but those that did were not sufficiently enthused to start the bush-fire effect which is the making of a bestseller.

The trouble with this is that there's no one person to blame, nothing to get fired-up about, or at. It's not a clean, agonising cut, it's a gradually realised nagging pain which leaves you downcast and debilitated. Your publisher will do her best: 'The figures may not be what we'd all hoped for, but then the market is very depressed . . . ', 'It's a little disappointing, when we all adored the book so much . . . ', 'Who knows why these things happen . . . ?', 'When you look at what's on the current bestseller list it makes you wonder if the world's gone mad . . . '

None of this helps. Their slight awkwardness with you is just an additional embarrassment you could live without. The plain fact is that this particular book didn't work as a blockbuster. So is it worth going for it all over again?

Only you can be the judge of that. For once, I'm sitting this one out. Your confidence will be dented, and whether you can repair it sufficiently to have another bash at a blockbuster is up to you.

What you *must* do is let this one go, and write another.

11

FOOL IF YOU THINK IT'S OVER

Once your blockbuster's been accepted, don't run away with the idea that your part in the process has ended. The most important part may be behind you, but your continuing involvement is essential to the book's success. You are about to learn one of the great truths of publishing: as a promotable product, a novel is indivisible from its author.

Promotion

With competition in the market-place so fierce, a book must be aggressively marketed and widely talked-about to fulfil its potential. In order for this to happen, both publisher and retailers must be fired up. Even an established author contemplating a change of direction will need skilful relaunching.

Writing is a solitary process relying on self-motivation. To emerge from the creative cocoon into the harsh light of day, not to mention the glare of publicity, and blow one's own trumpet goes against the grain for most writers. Rejection may stab you in the vitals, but self-promotion feels almost as uncomfortable. Carol Smith, who has spent her whole professional life representing authors she cares about and promoting their work, was initially uncharacteristically diffident at the prospect of doing the same for herself. This was not owing to false modesty, or doubts about her novel – she wholeheartedly believed in it, and knew others did too – but she simply could not imagine standing up in cold blood and extolling its merits and, by implication, her own talent as a writer. For writers with no experience of the business at all it can be even more painful.

Some genuinely never manage to conquer their fear and dis-taste for promotion. They either do as little as possible, on a rigorously selective basis, or refuse point-blank on the grounds that they don't care for it and their efforts would do more harm than good. In some of these cases the book does well anyway – in others the author's non-involvement is a real drawback.

Most authors learn what they need to do as they go along, and a great many of them find they enjoy promotion, simply because it is so different from the introspective isolation of writing. The most important thing to remember is that the book is yours – and if you can't take pride and pleasure in every stage of its career, then it will be harder for others to do so.

Attitude

With this in mind, cultivate the right attitude from the word go. From your very first dealings with your editor, let your enthusi-asm show. A positive approach is infectious, and fostering a good relationship with the publisher pays dividends all round. You're all on the same side – all these people are bringing their time, talents and skills to bear on your book, in the interests of making it a success. You'll make their job a lot easier and more enjoyable if you play your part.

This next bit is not for the sensitive, so turn the page now if you wish to avoid the risk of apoplexy.

Look your best. There, I've said it. I'm not suggesting you get poured into shoulder-pads and power heels if they're not your usual style – and more particularly if you're male – but when you first meet your publisher, make an effort. This is not only so that they form a favourable first impression, but so that you feel as good about yourself and as relaxed and confident as you possibly can. If that means the aforementioned sharp suit, then go for it. If you're more of a jeans and work-shirt sort of person, then that's fine too, but make the look as knock-out as you can. Remember you want to be the author, out of hundreds of authors, who will land the coveted television interview.

Self-promotion starts with self-knowledge. The injunction to

'Be yourself' which you will certainly have heard at your mother's knee, is surprisingly hard to follow, particularly in a way that will come over not just to one person but to a number of people at one time. You need to be able to accentuate the positive, and if not eliminate the negative then at least play it down as much as possible. If you've never heard yourself on tape, or seen yourself on video, now may be the time to do so. It will be dismaying, but instructive. Step back from yourself in order to see and hear what others see and hear. Keep calm. You are not Quasimodo, nor the Wicked Witch of the West. You are you, with family and friends who love you for all your many excellent qualities. You are about to have a book published. Clearly there are plenty of things you're doing right. But could you present yourself better?

The same 'stepping back' needs to happen with the book. No one seriously expects you to get up and announce that it's the most riveting, unputdownable and best-written book this century – and no one would believe it either. Value judgements are the publisher's (and, if you're lucky, the critic's) department. What you need to do is be unashamed and unembarrassed about your enthusiasm for the book – the original idea, its development, the research, the writing. What surprises were there along the way? What characters did you like best? What was easy to write? What was hard? Were you sorry to finish? Did any of the background material move, amuse or shock you? Are there any amusing stories connected with work on the book? These are areas that only the author herself is in a position to talk about. Take advantage of them. Get personal. Be passionate. Your belief in yourself and the book will come across – more precious than rubies, believe me. This is not an exercise in vanity, but in telling it like it is. Just think – all this time you've been slaving away over your labour of love. Now, at last, you've got the chance to talk about it. Enjoy it!

Your role in the mix

The author has a very distinct role in the promotional mix. A lot more than half the battle is understanding what that role is.

You're the most important person, the *sine qua non*. None of this would be taking place without your book. It follows therefore that you can afford to be humble, and accept that your book would not be going places were it not for the discernment and sagacity of this particular publisher. Acknowledge that the different departments working on your behalf are experts. Don't tell them their job. If your opinion is invited, then give it, honestly but politely, but don't expect it to be acted on, and certainly don't be miffed if it isn't.

A good example of this is the question of the book's cover. Note that I avoided the phrase 'vexed question'. Most authors have a moan from time to time about covers. They feel they've been misrepresented, or that their covers are dull/tasteless/uninformative/just plain wrong. It's a classic case of 'well, *you* do it then'. A tiny proportion of authors might be able to improve on the design, but most of us would make a proper pig's breakfast of it.

The only instance known personally to me where an author plainly had the edge was in the case of a friend of mine who had written the history of a well-known charity whose patron was the Princess of Wales. HRH had written the foreword, and my friend pointed out that the way was open for a cover featuring the Princess with a motherless child. Magazine research has shown that Di on the cover is good for several thousand extra sales. And yet the completed cover depicted dreary buildings in black and white, inanimate and depressing. Of course we'll never know what the sales figures would have been with HRH, but one is tempted to think it would have made a difference.

That, however, is the exception that proves the rule. Ninety-nine times out of a hundred the publisher's choice of cover is right. You may have thought of something cleverer and even more artistic, but in terms of visibility and selling the book, theirs will be more effective.

The cover is the first impression a prospective reader receives. As such, it is not simply an artistic representation of your story (though with luck it's that too) – it has to send out a clear, easily interpreted signal about the sort of book this is. The type of cover you have will speak volumes (sorry) about what's inside. The character of the artwork, lettering, colour are all designed to convey the message. It's also self-evident that this message must be plain not just at a distance of inches, but of feet, and if possible yards. Your brilliant title and what surrounds it must hit the target fair and square from the window, the shelf, the display table or wherever.

Also, I hate to tell you this, but at least one of the major book chains makes its stock selection exclusively by cover.

So don't, I implore you, be too picky about covers. You could be digging your own grave.

Selling

When it comes to selling, the field's wide open. There is no such thing as an author who over-promotes, provided she isn't a pain-in-the-butt. If you bear in mind that the purpose of the exercise is to win people over, engage their interest and predispose them to adore your novel, then you won't go far wrong. As for the people in the publisher's press and publicity department, they want an author they can fearlessly send out on the road to libraries, literary lunches, radio and television studios, bookshops, workshops, festivals and foreign parts, knowing that she'll put across her love and enthusiasm for the novel, make lots of fans and no enemies, and not run up expenses like the national debt.

The front-line troops in all this are the publisher's sales force. They are the ones at the sharp end, who have to enter the retail outlets armed only with a catalogue, a few covers and a spiel, and persuade a sceptical manager to order your book, preferably in numbers, instead of a similar title from another publisher. Having sold (or not sold) yours, they then have several other titles to sell. Next time you're in a bookshop and a publisher's rep comes in, hover close at hand – it's an education.

As the person with the second biggest stake in the book's success (after the publisher), you can never give the reps too much ammunition. Think about it. With anything up to a hundred titles to sell, twice a year, the likelihood of the rep having read your book is remote. He may have read a little of it. His wife may have read a little of it. Otherwise he's dependent on what he's told. You are probably not a 'name' author. The fact that the publisher is treating your book as a potential blockbuster is certainly a plus, but what the rep needs most is the combination only you can give him: inside knowledge and wholehearted belief in the book.

If you're invited to attend a sales conference, seize the opportunity with both hands, no matter how terrifying the prospect. The fact is that your presence, and almost anything you say, will be grist to the reps' mill. They'll already know – because they'll have been told – that your novel is a potential Big One. They won't have time to do more than glance at it – you're the one who can put fire in their bellies and light in their eyes so that they take the bookshops by storm. At the sales conference you'll probably be asked to speak for five to ten minutes. This is an exercise in getting the message across. Don't try and summarise the plot of your novel – say what the theme and background is, why you wanted to write it, why you enjoyed doing so, why you think others will enjoy reading it. If you've got time, read a *short* passage out loud, a few lines that will give the flavour of the whole. But only if a few such lines present themselves as ideal. It's the taste and feel of your book you want to convey, and what it's about in broad terms. This doesn't have to be a polished speech, but to be effective you should take it seriously and marshal your thoughts beforehand, so that you use the short time at your disposal effectively. Think what you want to hear when someone else is recommending a book to you – the kind of thing that makes you prick up your ears, and kindles your enthusiasm. Express your solidarity with the efforts of the publisher, and your willingness to do whatever you can to help promote the book.

The dreaded form

Some time prior to publication you will receive a form from the publisher which requires to know more about you and your book than you actually know yourself. Why does that simple question about 'interests and hobbies' reduce me to feeling like a friendless, brain-dead recluse whose idea of a wild night is watching *Come Dancing?*

Do your best, though, because take it from me it gets worse. Even more questions and even larger spaces are allowed for information about the novel. Can you summarise what it's about? Write a 'blurb' for it? Can you suggest ways in which it might be promoted? Any specialist groups or organisations whom it might be worth approaching? Does it have any regional interest? Your first instinct will be that the answer to all these is 'no'. Crestfallen, you may even feel that the novel is doomed to failure, because there isn't a living soul out there to whom it's likely to appeal.

Think again. Begin by having a go at the blurb – it's fiendishly hard, but it will force you to 'sell' your novel (not least to yourself, as I suggested in the chapter on planning), and it's a useful exercise in storming your barriers of reserve and false modesty. If you can write anything approaching your own blurb, you're halfway to being able to promote the book. Don't worry too much about the other stuff. If the novel's set in Manchester then by all means make a virtue of the fact. If it is about high finance, or a Highland regiment, or colonial East Africa, make a point of saying so. But the most vital asset of a blockbuster is broad appeal not parochial interest.

One for the road

When the publicity department, on fire with enthusiasm for you and your book, speak of media attention, television chat shows, radio arts programmes, breakfast interviews and Sunday magazine profiles (and that's quite separate from the reviews by the yard which will inevitably come your way), they are neither flannelling nor practising to deceive. All these things are possible – but extremely unlikely.

Radio

Radio is very likely to come your way – particularly local radio, both commercial and BBC. The form here is that in nine cases out of ten you'll be on a music/magazine programme where the presenter (who will also be flicking switches, banging buttons, playing cassettes and tapes, selecting jingles, and timing and introducing news, weather and travel slots) will have read the publisher's press release, but not the book. She'll probably have a copy to hand, and may have glanced at the first few pages just before you arrived. You can therefore expect that if specific references to the text are made, they will be from those early pages. Otherwise, conversation will be in broad terms. How did you start writing? Where do you get your ideas from? What made you write this particular book? Tell us a bit about it. Is it autobiographical at all? Do you work to a set routine? Have you got any tips for would-be writers who may be listening?

Don't get stuffy about the kind of questions. They provide you with a much better platform for saying things that will sell your books than more picky and specific ones. All the same rules apply. Be yourself. Put across your enthusiasm and interest. Don't be frightened to mention the things that you found difficult – they make your success all the more impressive. As with your novel, it's feelings that we all have in common and can identify with. Let your feelings show.

In a live interview you won't have long, and the time you do have will be interrupted by music and the other slots we mentioned. If they tell you you're going to be on for half an hour, you'll probably only speak for about 12-15 minutes of that, top whack. The presenter wants you to talk, but it's her job to keep you to the point and moving along at a reasonable rate. Talk to her, the other person, not to the microphone. Don't hesitate to use the politician's trick of saying chiefly what you want to say rather than precisely answering the question. The presenter wants a lively, interesting show. Think in advance about things like helpful tips, what the book's main appeal is, your working methods, and what's in the pipeline. On this type of programme no one's trying to catch you out, you're there to help them fill the time, and in return they help you to sell your book.

A pre-recorded interview will be more leisurely, partly because it's not live, and partly because it won't contain all that music, travel, weather and so on. The chances are that there will be a greater concentration on the contents of the book, and you'll have time to talk in a little more depth about it, and yourself. The interviewer will have told you what kind of programme the feature will be used in, and what sort of audience it has. Here again, it's most unlikely that you'll be 'got at'. If you are lobbed any awkward or hostile questions (it's commercial but is it art? do books like these stop other books being published? is this a case of never mind the quality feel the width?), don't rise to the bait. Don't be rushed – give yourself time to think. Firmly but politely dismiss the premise, and refer back to your own inspiration, motivation and involvement in the novel. Value judgements are for others to make – you simply wrote the very best book you could, and hope it will reach as many people as possible.

The third type of interview is 'down the line' – over the phone. This can be live or recorded and is my personal un-favourite because you can't avail yourself of any of the usual signs and signals given out by your interrogator – body language, appearance, gesture and expression. The two of you are working blind. The one comfort is that she's in the same position as you, and suffering from all the same disadvantages. You are anonymous, so be bold.

Press

Press interviews are far less nerve-racking to undergo, and that may well be why the resulting article is so often a shock. Did I *really* say that? And (worse) if I did say it, is that what I meant? Cold print irons out nuances of meaning and expression, and frequently divorces a remark from its context, with embarrassing consequences. Here again, the interviewer may not be trying to catch you out or trap you into saying something foolish – but she won't be trying to protect you, either. And when she's writing up the interview she'll very naturally want to make it read like an interesting story with a particular angle. You can hardly blame her for highlighting some remarks, playing down or omitting others, and colouring the whole thing with her subjective view (it's just what you did with your novel, after all). If you feel violently that you have been misrepresented, think carefully before making any kind of hoohah. 'Never complain, never explain' is sound advice. Most people reading about you in a paper or magazine will simply register the fact that you – and your book – are there on the page. Unless the journalist is making you out to be an axe-murderer or claiming that your book is seditious, semi-literate garbage, put up with it. In fact, put up with it anyway.

One especially effective weapon of the press interviewer is The Silence. This relies on the fact that most people abhor a vacuum, feel discomforted by it, and will usually jump into it – with both feet. Prattling on is the enemy of the interviewee. As one who could prattle for Britain, I know whereof I speak. When you've said what you were going to say, stop. This is not a social conversation, you have no responsibility for keeping it going. Wait. Out wait the interviewer if need be. That way there will be far less likelihood of your saying something idiotic or damaging.

Television

The most sought-after opportunity, and the least likely of all. Even given that she wishes to speak to someone who has written a book, a chat show host, confronted with a straight choice between you and a troubled film star who has penned her autobiography, will go for the film star every time – or the controversial politician, the brilliant sportsman, the woman who married a headhunter, and the tug-of-love father. A new novel by an unknown writer, no matter how earth-shaking, is not, if you'll pardon the expression, a story. Though of course you yourself may be: very occasionally a rags-to-riches publishing tale catches the hardboiled media imagination, but one such tale goes a long way, and the chances are you won't be the lucky one. Television coverage is about as probable as being struck by lightning.

If you're lucky enough to be invited on television, then remember the basics – look as good as is consistent with feeling comfortable; be yourself; remember why you love the book and enjoyed writing it; talk to the individual, not the camera, the crew or the unseen thousands.

Public speaking

It won't give you great pleasure. Not to begin with anyway. I believe there are statistics which show that public speaking is one of
the major stress-generating activities. But if you are someone who
takes to it, or who can at least make a fist of doing it from time to
time, it's a great way to promote.

Let's be clear about this. The first thing you want an audience
to do is like you. To this end take care with the appearance, and
this means its suitability, not its degree of drop-dead glamour. The
speaker is a hired gun. Make an effort to look good and, more
importantly, appropriate. Don't guess what sort of thing to wear –
ask. You might for instance think that you can't go wrong with a
little black dress, and wind up, as I did, indistinguishable from the
waitresses . . .

Take advantage of any spare time before the function to circu-
late and gauge the mood of the meeting. If you're in the slightest
doubt about any particular reference, or joke, leave it out. People
won't miss what they don't know about, but if you offend, you're
doomed.

Ask how long your hosts want you to speak for and keep to
time, or just inside it. You can always invite questions, but nothing's worse than a speaker who outstays her welcome. The first
public speaking engagement I ever did was a literary luncheon at
the Cutlers' Hall in Sheffield: linen-fold panelling, squadrons of
chandeliers, paintings as big as soccer pitches, and an audience
comprising mayor and corporation, city fathers, and six hundred
ladies hatted, furred and jewelled to the nines.

'Don't worry,' said my neighbour, a jolly alderman with a big
moustache and a high colour, 'you could stand up and fart and
they'd still love you.' How I wished I could believe him. There
were four speakers: a famous actor, a famous film producer, a
duchess – and me. I was a complete newcomer, and seven months
pregnant. The speakers were put on in ascending order of importance, so I had to kick off. A toastmaster in hunting pink adjusted
the microphone and put a little box with perspex buttons on the
table alongside my untouched coffee. 'The speaker's friend,'
murmured the toastmaster, all unction and up-yours. 'If you go

139

past five minutes the light will flash.'

Those ladies will never know how lucky they were that I didn't give birth right there at the top table in the Cutlers' Hall. My speech was over in one and a half minutes.

What makes public speaking difficult, winking lights aside, is that there is no one else in charge, to prompt, prod and guide you. It's like jumping off the high diving-board. As you rise, dry-mouthed and damp-palmed, to your feet, you find yourself thinking that if you'd wanted to be an actress, a politician or a stand-up comic you wouldn't have written a flaming novel. But anyway, here you are, so you'd better accept that it goes with the territory.

Be prepared, chiefly about what you're going to say. You should aim for a good opening shot; a complimentary reference to your hosts and the occasion; an introduction to what you're going to say; some anecdotes (amusing, dramatic, affecting, preferably a selection) on the subject of writing, and your novel in particular (that's why they asked you); another reference to the organisers; and a great get-out. Whatever time you've been allowed, these basic building blocks hold good. With experience, you'll accumulate a whole mental crateful of these modules, and will be able to snap a selection together to suit a particular audience or occasion.

To begin with, you'll want to write them down. Then you can either read the speech off like an essay (no shame in this, better a first-class speech read out than a stammering shambles without notes) but don't forget to maintain plenty of eye-contact; you can make yourself some cue-cards (the most usual method); you can learn the whole damn thing off by heart; or you can do as I do and fly by the seat of the pants – I have enough material these days not to fear drying up, and because I'm short-sighted and prefer not to wear specs when I speak, I don't like being tied to bits of paper.

Make sure you're audible – speak up and look up (eye-contact again), and don't get frozen – use gestures, be natural. There are quite enough stuffed shirts, tailors' dummies and crunching bores on the speaking circuit. If you've got something to say, enjoy saying it – then they'll enjoy listening to you.

Shifting product

A live audience which has just heard you speak compellingly about your work will be predisposed to buy a book. If the occasion is a literary lunch or Dinner then the organisers will almost certainly have arranged for a local bookshop to sell copies of the speakers' books afterwards. Approach this in a realistic way. If the other speakers are celebrities in their own right, people will be more likely to want their autographs than yours (that's the only reason for buying the book here, after all), and if the other books are in paperback and yours is in hardback, the same applies. It's not only about selling the book on the night, it's about fixing you, as an author, in people's minds, so that next time they see something of yours on the shelf they'll select it in preference to someone else's.

If you're invited to a library you'll have more time and a pleasantly relaxed atmosphere. There will be a bookstall present, but a library audience is not the same as a lunch or dinner crowd, and may not be so free-spending.

It's on those occasions when you have been invited privately, i.e. not through the publisher, that it pays to be shameless. You as the author can obtain all your titles at an author discount of a third on the retail price. Keep a supply in. When you're invited to speak, ask if you may bring with you some books to sell. It's most unusual for this offer to be refused. I've sold as many as fifty books in an evening. Once again, the purpose is not only the profit to yourself – which is quite small – but the consciousness-raising effect of having all your titles on display, and the opportunity it provides for talking to the customers. If you have books in stock, it's also good PR to offer a signed copy for the raffle, tombola, auction or whatever's going on.

Photographs

What can I say? I don't know anyone who likes having their picture taken, or who doesn't wail with shame and outrage at the result, especially if it's published for all to see. In the case of the mugshot on the jacket, it's quite likely that the publisher will arrange to have a set of photos taken, especially since they're backing you as a bestseller. It's not a bad idea to ask for a look at the contact sheet, and purchase for yourself some prints of the ones you like. That way you're forearmed on those occasions when a journalist says, 'Do you have any photographs of yourself?'

Otherwise it's my experience that almost without exception a photo's quality is in inverse proportion to the amount of time it takes to set up. In many cases this is also reflected in the cost, which can be pretty galling. I'm usually pleasantly surprised by photos in local newspapers, and on the verge of shooting myself over ones in glossy magazines where I'm depicted 'at my desk' (usually not the real thing, but mocked up in a more salubrious corner of the house), face in a rictus, shoulders rigid, eyes glassy and hands unconvincingly poised over a lifeless keyboard. By far my nicest author-photos in years were taken recently at my local high-street studio. Both the cost and time involved were minimal. (Is there a conspiracy about just how difficult it is to take pictures? I think we should be told.) You may think you're not vain, but when you realise that an unflattering photograph of you is about to go out on thousands of book jackets, and be used in endless posters and press handouts, the sleeping giant of vanity will stir and shake its hoary locks. I should let sleeping giants lie, if I were you.

Horror stories

Book-promotion's a bit like childbirth – it may be uncomfortable, but it's worth it in the end. It's also a great shared rite of passage among published authors, and no discussion of it is complete without a clutch of accompanying horror stories. As light relief I offer one or two of my own here.

Book fairs

Attendance at book fairs has to be one of the swiftest levellers of all time. Trailing clouds of glory and high on your publisher's confidence, you arrive like John Wayne – and depart like Mickey Rooney. You didn't know there were that many books in the *world,* since time *began,* let alone published this year. The air vibrates with the accumulated batsqueaks of a million authorial egos all clamouring for attention. Publishers cluster on their stands like knife-gangs looking out for victims. The author lucky – or un-lucky – enough to have been invited along has a curious, passive role. You're there to join the team for a drink, to be seen, to talk up the product, and to gape disbelievingly at your author-photo blown up to poster size, and wonder why you allowed it.

Book fairs (and remember the poor publisher is there for the duration) are boring, airless, unhealthy and claustrophobic. But they happen. All you can do is try not to be put off your stroke. The fact that millions of titles are assembled under one roof does not mean that your novel is in direct competition with those mil-lions of titles. Only with some of them. Keep both a sense of proportion and your cool. Put it down to experience. Only a very few authors are vouchsafed the salutary experience of the book fair, so be pleased you're one of them.

Interviews from hell

Worse than the book fair, because more personal, are some of the things you'll find yourself doing in the name of promotion. On one overseas tour I wound up on one of those daytime television shopping channels, sandwiched between the men's casual wear and the personalised storage jars . . . A little later on the same tour I was invited to fill a slot on a country and western radio channel. The presenter was a hunky young man in a plaid shirt and stetson. To my astonishment he appeared to have read the book. 'You wanna know the part I liked best?' he enquired, on air. I did, I said, I really did. 'It was the part where the couple were rolling around on those freshly laundered sheets like seals on the polar ice-cap,' he told me with a grin and a wink. I had absolutely no idea what he was talking about. Couples certainly did do some rolling about in my book, but I had no knowledge of this particular striking simile. I was relieved to get out of the studio, and be whisked up the hill to the local television station to take part in what my accompanying publicist referred to as a 'proper arts programme'. In make-up my face was scrubbed out and replaced with a more all-purpose one. In the studio you could tell this was serious stuff because the set consisted of two uncomfortable chairs on plinths, and a plant. The presenter entered – suit, horn-rims, clipboard. The green light went on. The camera rolled. One or two serious questions were asked. And then came the one I'd thought never to hear again:

'Wanna know the part I liked best? It was the part where the couple were rolling around on the freshly laundered . . . '

Again it meant nothing to me. But he did. It was the same man.

No-shows

Another downer is the non-appearance of the expected audience. This has happened to me twice, both times at libraries. It's absolutely no reflection on the library staff, who had done all they reasonably could. But perhaps it's no coincidence that on both occasions the libraries concerned were huge, gothic inner-city structures, as user-friendly as oil rigs and about as accessible. I've never been able to work out why people should want to set out at night, in the dark, in winter, to a place where there is no parking within a quarter of a mile and which can only be reached by braving a threatening underpass or crossing a dual carriageway, to hear an author speak for an hour.

On the first occasion, no one came at all. Actually, that's much easier. Once the situation became obvious (the chief librarian had begun dragging in the night-cleaners), I simply suggested we cut our losses and go to the pub. The poor staff must have been miserably embarrassed, and probably had a riotous time once I'd left, but at least I didn't actually have to do the talk in any formal sense.

The second time, I did. I arrived at the library to find enough chairs for over a hundred people, each with a programme on the seat. I was due to start at eight. At ten past there was still only me, the staff, and the man from the local paper. As I opened my mouth to suggest a pint, and so put everyone out of their misery, footsteps were heard on the stairs. I had an audience!

It was my brother, his wife, and a friend. Never have I been so touched by family solidarity, or so keen to strangle them. We sat in the corner of the huge room, backs to the platform, and I did my number to seven people.

Death by signing

In the public humiliation stakes, all of the afore-mentioned fade into insignificance beside the shame and horror of the signing session.

If you're ever asked to do one of these, just stop before accepting and ask yourself: 'Are people going to want my autograph?' It's the only criterion worth bothering with. No matter how marvellous and brilliant your novel, most people will buy it as a result of leisurely choice. Unless you are already one of a rarefied handful of celebrity authors (which if you're reading this book I suggest you aren't, yet), or a celebrity in your own right (Joan Collins, Margaret Thatcher), forget it. Why should people spend £14.99, and stand in a queue, for your autograph? Get real.

If you do accept, be ready to sit at a table trying to look serene and composed while the entire world ignores you. Like some over-the-hill lady of the night in her shop window in Amsterdam, you try to pull the passers-by, but they stay resolutely unpulled. They don't just ignore you, they're actually embarrassed by your naked need. The only ones who aren't embarrassed are the ones who think you work in the shop, and ask you where they can find Judith Krantz.

There are steps you can take, though they've all been tried before. You can alert your friends and relatives in the area that you'll be in the shop, but this presupposes that they haven't supportively gone out and bought the book already. You can try to get a local newspaper to run a story on your imminent ordeal, and literally plead with the public to turn up, but this trick can only be carried off at infrequent intervals, and probably by 'name' authors who don't need it anyway. Or you can refuse.

I recommend refusing.

And does any of it matter?

Yes. It does. I told you at the beginning of this book that I was going to give you an author's perspective on the whole process of writing a blockbuster, and I'd be failing to deliver if I didn't warn you about what is consequent upon the writing.

Also, the business of publicity and promotion can have a very positive and constructive bearing on your subsequent writing. Sweating over forms, wooing the sales force, squirming in studios, fencing with journalists, dying in bookshops and weeping over photographs are all learning experiences. You can't write if you don't engage with life. Besides which, all the talking about your book, and what went into producing it, will focus your mind. When you go back to your writing, you'll know more about it, and yourself, than you did before. You'll have a stronger sense of your own identity, and for the blockbuster writer that can only be good.

So don't be precious about promotion. It's your book you're selling.

POSTSCRIPT

Like every writer you are, ultimately, on your tod. But that's no reason to feel bleak or isolated. On the contrary you should feel good about it.

Because when all's said and done the only person who can write your blockbuster is you. It's your unique vision, voice and imagination that will inform the story; your energy, enthusiasm and sheer bloody-mindedness that can take it to the top. Take all the advice you can lay your hands on, including this book, but remember it is *only* advice. Some of it may provide the tools you need to make the writing of a blockbuster easier, and some you may reject. That's as it should be. The important thing is that you give it due consideration before moving on.

I wish you all the luck in the world. And I envy you the excitement of your first blockbuster, the angst and the hard graft as well as the elation. I do hope that if this book provides you with even a smidgin of help, or inspiration, or amusement you'll let me know.

Remember: inspiration is what happens to you when you're busy writing.

And don't let anyone rain on your parade.

INDEX

148

INDEX